LIVING SYSTEMS: THEORY AND APPLICATION

LIVING SYSTEMS: THEORY AND APPLICATION

TAGE FRANDBERG

Nova Science Publishers, Inc.
Huntington, New York

Library of Congress Cataloging-in-Publication Data
Frandberg, Tage.
Living systems : theory and application / by Tage Frandberg.
p. cm.
Includes bibliographical references and index.
ISBN 1-56072-915-5
1. Life. 2. System theory. I. Title.
BD435.F66 2001 2001023563
113'.8--dc21 CIP

227 Main Street, Suite 100
Huntington, New York 11743
Tele. 631-424-6682 Fax 631-424-4666
e-mail: Novascience@earthlink.net
Web Site: http://www.nexusworld.com/nova

Printed in the United States of America

CONTENTS

INTRODUCTION

As an introduction I have illustrated alternative ways of how we can think of our relations to nonliving systems and our environment, and how these are described by different subject areas. I also discuss the philosophy behind the theory of Living Systems and make comparisons with other theories/ideas. I subsequently discuss issues concerning attitudes to the building of models and their qualities of model building and their qualities, as well as cybernetics, entropy, values and validity, quality of life, and "cause, effect and emergence". It has been important display these points of view at the outset because of the fact that they are preconditions for my motive to apply the theory of Living Systems. Finally, I by means of examples based on simulation demonstrate the application of Living Systems, and also show how these can be founded on the Internet.

Chapter 1

LIVING AND NONLIVING SYSTEMS

What is living? How did the living come into existence and how is "living" characterized? How can we imagine relations between living and nonliving systems? There are different responses to these questions but as yet none which gives a complete and generally accepted answer. Examples are to be found in Nicolis and Prigogine (1989) and in Herrman (1989). "It is true that great strides have been and are being made in, for example, molecular biology in order to describe the line between living and nonliving systems. In the field of Physics great strides have also been made in order to bring us nearer to an explanation of the emergence and composition of matter."

(Peter Nilsson 1992 p. 178) "Today we do not know if there is a clear boundary between life and nonlife seemingly there is not either a clear boundary between consciousness and unconsciousness. Is an ant or an amoeba only a small machine constructed of organic molecules; or are they beings with a rudimentary consciousness; or perhaps both?"

Miller has defined living systems (Miller 1978 p. 18): "Every concrete system which does not have the characteristics of a living system is a nonliving system. Nonliving systems constitute the general case of concrete systems, of which living systems are a very special case." According to Miller General Living Systems Theory (Miller 1978 p. 41) (GLST), is an interdisciplinary approach which is characterized by the following

The most general form of systems theory is a set of logical or mathematical statements about all conceptual systems.

One subset of this concerns all concrete systems.

One subset concerns the very special and very important living systems described, i.e. general living systems theory.

The question of the difference between living and nonliving is here according to the system's view seen as depending on the relationships between living and nonliving systems — e.g. when birds can not find places to build their nests, when forests for example are damaged. The nest is a nonliving thing but in connection with a bird the nest is decisive for the bird's survival. As a consequence one is obliged to see the survival of the birds as a living system consisting of nonliving and living systems.

In "Basic Concepts" Miller has given an account of structures and processes in Living Systems which is the basis for the application of the simulation. Miller (1978 p. 18); the content in the paragraphs has been shortened here

(a) They are open systems with significant inputs, throughputs, and outputs of various sorts of matter-energy and information.
(b) They maintain a steady state of negentropy even though entropic changes occur in them as they do everywhere else.
(c) They have more than a certain degree of complexity.
(d) They either contain genetic material composed of deoxiribonucleie acid (DNA), presumably descended from some primordial DNA common to all life, or have a charter.
(e) They are largely composed of an aqueous suspension of macromolecules, proteins constructed from about 20 amino acids and other characteristic organic compounds, and may also include nonliving components.
(f) They have a decider
(g) They also have certain other specific critical subsystems or they have symbiotic or parasitic relationships.
(h) These subsystems are integrated together to form actively self-regulating, developing, unitary systems with purpose and goals.
(i) They can exist only in a certain environment.

Living Systems is limited to the subset of living systems: cells, organs, organisms, groups, organizations, societies and supranational systems. Miller sees the earth as a mixed system, a combination of a living and nonliving system over and above the supranational system. (Margulis, Sagan 1995 p.

177) sees the biosphere as a hierarchical system. They write "Nor did life stop at complex cells and multicellular beings. It went on, forging societies and communities and the living biosphere itself."

HIERARCHICAL SYSTEMS

In Living Systems (Miller 1978 p. 25) the universe is described as

> "a hierarchy of systems, each more advanced or "higher" level made of systems of lower levels. The systems range from atoms composed of particles to "higher" levels of systems which may be of mixed composition, living and nonliving. They include ecological systems, planets, solar systems, galaxies, and so forth."

An illustration of how hierarchies can be used to portray the Universe and its incomprehensible distances is in the following quotation from "Mapping the Universe" by Stephen D. Landy in Scientific American June 1999 p. 30, which shows how galaxies form into progressively larger groupings.

> "As the viewer moves out from the Milky Way galaxy to the entire observable universe, clumpiness finally gives way to smoothness each sphere is 10 times wider - and therefore 1000 times more voluminous-than the previous one. A galaxy is a lump of stars, gas, dust and unclassified "dark matter". It agglomerates with other galaxies to form galaxy clusters, the largest bodies in the universe held together by gravity. The clusters, in turn, are clumped together into superclusters and walls, separated by voids of nearly empty intergalactic space. Up to some scale, thought to be around 100 million light-years, they form a fractal pattern - that is, they are equivalently clumpy on every scale. But between this scale and the size of the observable universe, the clumpiness gives way to near uniformity". The hierarchy is described by denoting light years

10^5 light–years galaxy, 10^6 light–years groups of galaxies,
10^7 light–years cluster, 10^8 light-years supercluster, 10^9 light years walls and voids, 10^{10} light–years universe.

Stephen Jay Kline (Kline 1995 p. 107) has a Figure which illustrates the above figures.

Arbitrary number indicating the level of size	Biological forms	Human- made objects,systems	Natural physical objects
9			Unknown
8			Universe
7		Space probes, space communications	Galaxies
6			Solar systems
5	Global ecologies	Space systems, United Nations	Stars, planets
4	Marine ecologies	Large sociotechnical systems, systems of transport, national governments	Continents, oceans
3[a]	Local ecologies, forests	Socitechnical systems (human-made ecologies	
2[a]	Clans, herds, tribes	Large, hardware, (buildings, machines)	
1[a]	Families	Simple hardware (artifacts, hand tools, furniture)	
0[a]	Multicellular plants, animals	Materials (steel, semiconductors, etc.)	Aggregations of atoms and molecules
–1	Unicellular plants,animals		
–2	Organells, macromolcules, proteins	Semiconductors circuits	Individual molecules
–3			Individual atoms
–4			Subatomic particles
–5			Unknown

Figure 1:1 The Hierarchy of Constitution: A Taxonomy of objects Arranged by Size and Nature. a Levels 0, 1, 2, and/or 3 are sometimes called the "classical level, referring to classical physics."

If we look at subatomic levels, we can consider the following quotation taken from Igor D. Novikov (1998 p. 168) "All processes in the Universe are the results of these four types (gravity and electromagnetism which we know from everyday life, and two kinds of short range nuclear power, week power and strong power of interaction. What actually happens in these interactions? What is the most important thing about them? Particles interact via the exchange of other particles – carriers of interactions. Each of the four types of interaction has its own carriers. The electromagnetic interaction is mediated by the photon, its 'carrier', and the gravitational interaction is mediated by the graviton. These two always move at the speed of light and have no mass of their own. Physicists say that their mass (another expression is 'their rest mass') is zero."

The weak interaction also has its 'carriers'. These particles that physicists call 'vector bosons'. The essential difference between these and the photon and the graviton is that they are extremely massive: about a hundred times heavier than the proton. Because the carriers are so heavy, the weak interaction is only possible at extremely short distances. This distance is about a thousand times shorter than the size of an atomic nucleus. Recall that a nucleus is about a hundred thousand times smaller than the atom. Novikov (1998 p. 171) writes that: "The properties of this world are closely tied to the properties of the infinitely large Universe." and he thereby demonstrates connections between the subatomic level and levels at the borders of the Universe.

On the basis of these illustrations of the lowest and the highest levels, we can as does Peter Nilsson (1993 p. 70), imagine, there being an affinity between living and nonliving systems. All living things have their origin in the nonliving – this is a cosmic paradox, which science even today has not succeeded in resolving entirely. Peter Nilsson continues: In some way or another – we do not know – how the human brain can detect patterns which resemble or simulate this order of the Universe (Nilsson 1993 p. 74) There seem to be traces of a "program" which makes the world to be what it is. As physical beings we represent the laws of astrophysics and nuclear physics, matter and power fields. In some sense these laws must also be in operation when we think, dream, write poetry, and carry on research. Our consciousness, our thoughts and all sensations which have room in our souls (*what this does can now imply: my remark*) have something to tell us about the Universe. But we do not know exactly what it is.

Murray Gell-Mann writes in (Murray Gell-Mann Swedish ed. second ed.) that some quantum cosmologists tend to talk about an “antropic principle” which demands that the conditions within the universe can be seen with consistent with the existence of human beings. A mild version of this principle limits itself to saying that the specific branch of history where we are has qualities which are decisive for the existence of our planet and enable human life to flourish here. In this form the “antropic principle” is obvious. But the perspective entailed by the adoption of this principle in its strongest form would probably imply that certain interpretations of both the dynamic and the primordial conditions of the universe, and in some degree form the basic laws in such a way that it is seen as inevitable that human beings arose. Gell-Mann does not find such an idea worth discussing; he says rather than some mystical “antropic principle”, we are in fact looking at conventional questions within the framework of theoretical science concerning the conditions which are required in order for complex adaptive systems to arise and develop at different junctures through history and in different places, given that the fundamental theory for elementary particles and the original state of the universe.

Below I give motives for seeing the Earth as a living system.

While it will lack subsystems it can nevertheless be worthwhile to study the Earth as a highest level, because the absence of these subsystems will show under which limitations we live.

As an example of a hierarchy which depicts subject areas as well as systems levels I have chosen a figure where disciplines are connected to the different levels – *Figure 1:1*

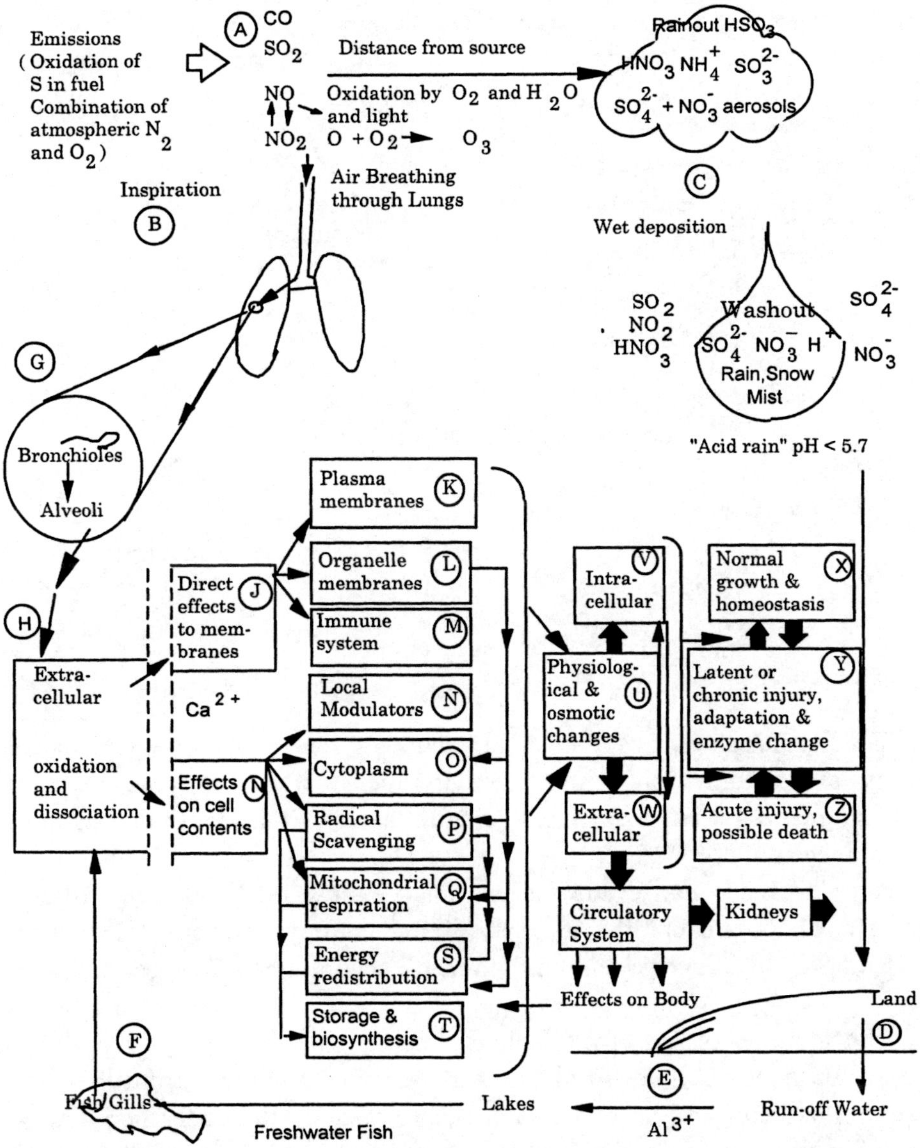

Figure 1:2 Where the levels of, cell, organ, organism and the Earth are illustrated in an interaction. Wellburn (1988)

Living Systems can be described by nine levels by *Figure 1:2*

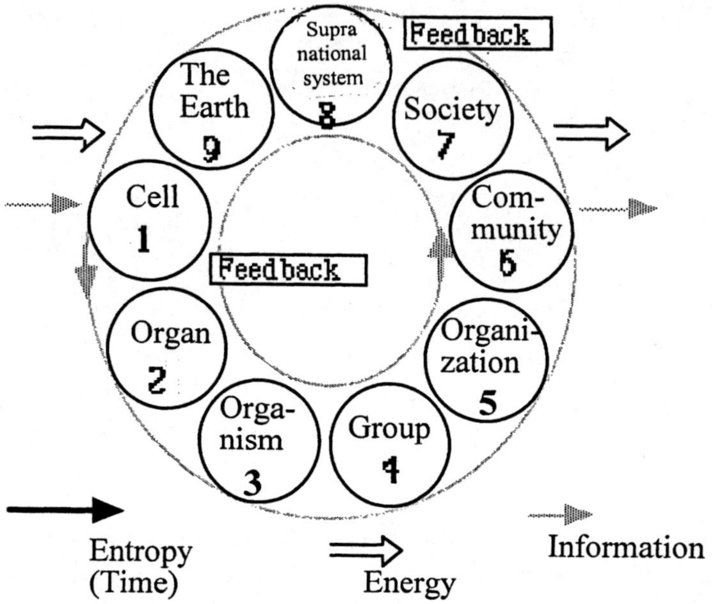

Figure 1:3 shows the nine levels the cell – the Earth.

The Earth is studied as a practically closed system (which only exchanges energy and information with its environment) which is going towards increasing entropy. Feedback lines go from the cell to the Earth and from the Earth to the cell.

A living being can evade the entropic degradation of its own structure only. It cannot prevent the increase of the entropy of the whole system, consisting of its structure and environment" according to Georgescu-Roegen (1971)

The increase of entropy which is assumed to take place according to *Figure 1:2* does not stem from the increase of heat coming from the living system, this being only a minor part. Approximately the difference between incoming solar energy and reflected energy is 53 %. 8 % is reflected by the atmosphere, 16 % is absorbed by the atmosphere, 20 % is reflected by clouds, 5 % is absorbed by clouds, and 5 % is reflected by the Earth's surface. Gribbin (1990 p. 130) refers to measurements which say that 153 watts per square meter represents the warming of the Earth by the greenhouse effect. The non-usable heat emanating from living systems is only a minor part. But the problem is that if the reflection of energy from the Earth is diminished by air pollution and the Earth's temperature is therefore increased and the ozone layer depleted the survival of living systems is threatened. The concept of entropy is dealt with in further detail in Chapter 8.

SUBJECT AREAS

If we proceed to an overview of our knowledge from the highest to the lowest level, we can look at a figure from "The hierarchy of Constitution, with the Location of a Number of Disciplines Indicated" in Stephen Jay Kline's book "Conceptual Foundations for Multidisciplinary Thinking"(1995 p. 108).

There is no discipline shown above the level of the Universe, nor any below the subatomic particles. This figure shows, that we cannot clearly define our knowledge of the unknown as also Peter Nilsson shows. Kline closes the chapter by depicting hierarchically thinking: "hierarchy is a nearly ubiquitous structural feature of systems, concepts, communication, and thought. In order to understand the structure of inert systems, living systems, books, concepts, communications and many other matters, we need the concept of hierarchy." This is the overall hierarchy of constitution as *Figure 1:3* illustrates. General Living Systems Theory is a theory which aims to facilitate communication and apply knowledge from the different disciplines within systems thinking

In the light of the fact that there are kinds of systems thinking which differs from Living Systems it seems desirable to anchor the application of Living Systems to its philosophical background. The above-mentioned examples illustrate a hierarchical view and approach to classification. In the next chapter I will consider how reality can be seen taking as a point of departure the philosophy of Alfred N. Whitehead.

Size (as in Fig. 7-1)	Representative objects from Fig. 7-1	Disciplines
9	Unknown	
8	Universe	Astrophysics
7	Galaxies	Astronomy
6	Solar systems	Astronomy
5	Stars, planets	Astronomy, astronautics
4	Continents, oceans	
3	Geologic features (mountains, valleys etc., including human-made ecologies, nations)	Geology, ecology, navigation, seamanship, aeronautics, forestry, marine biology, agriculture, economics, political science, grad. business, public health, urban studies, law, engineering economic systems, operations research, history, geography food research, public policy.....
2	Groups of people, large hardware	Engineering (many branches), education, feminist studies, English, art, math, ethnolgy, sociology, humanities, cumputer science, commuic-tions,.....
1	Families, colonies, simple hardware	Psychology, ethnology, languages, linguistics, paleoanthropology.....
0	Multicellular plants, animals	Zoology, botany, anatomy, psychology, biology, statistics, medicine (many branches),...
–1	Unicellular plants, animals	Parasitology, biology
–2	Individual molecules	Materials science, chemistry, biochemistry
–3	Individual atoms	Atomic physics
–4	Subatomic particles	
–5	Unknown	

Figure 1:4 The Hierarchy of Constitution, with the Location of Disciplines Indicated. Note that a number of discplines also apply adjacent to those shown. Taken from (Kline 1995. Figure 7-2 p. 108)

Chapter 2

PHILOSOPHY AND LIVING SYSTEMS THEORY

INTRODUCTION

Anders Pilz, an historian specialising in the history of ideas and also a Catholic priest, writes in "The World of Medieval Learning (1998) Swedish ed." (My translation). As early as the 12th century nominalists and realists were discussing ideas of reality. According to the nominalists only individuals represent reality, while genus and species are founded on a psychological process: we observe certain similarities between individuals and put them together according to these similarities. These conceptions have no reality outside the brain. This theory which in a proper meaning ought to be called conceptualism is named nominalism. William Ockham (approx. 1240-1349) denied everything else but substance and quality real existence. Relations are nothing which "exist" separately from two things and the person who is thinking about how these two things are related to each other. It is the abstractions of the language which mislead us to think that universal concepts, the categories and "formalities" should be something outside the brain.

If one is to show the whole contrasts in one formula, it will be this one; do the universal concepts exist as a reality in their own right, outside and independent of human thought? Is there a necessary connection between language and reality? Do we force the structure of language onto reality? This connection between reality and linguistic expression exists at the most fundamental level, and although the different languages entail that this connection is realised in different ways there is an eternal and unchanging connection between "mode of being" and "mode" of expression.

Points of View of Alfred N. Whitehead's Philosophy

It is not fully adequate to represent Whitehead's philosophy by using only certain selected parts/quotations but, I will nonetheless try to find a thread which in my opinion, influenced Living Systems. (Miller 1978) begins the preface to Living Systems by quoting from (Whitehead 1925) and concludes his book with a quotation from (Whitehead 1929, 1978 p. 215) "each actual entity is itself only describable as an organic process. It repeats in microcosm what the universe is in macrocosm. It is a process proceeding from phase to phase, each phase being the real basis from which its successor proceeds".

I would like to quote (Leclerc 1961 p. 12) "It is the particular function of philosophy to make explicit the schemes of ideas (established and newly emergent) which guide thought in the various specialist inquiries and in the various fields of applied sociology." This last paragraph is, according to my view, valid not only for sociology but for other subject areas as well.

As a beginning I wish to show how the ideas examined above can be applied to the Universe in Whitehead (Whitehead 1929, ed. 1978 p. 215) where he sees "the universe as in a rhythmical pulsation, from potentiality to actuality, and from actuality to potentiality, from the many to the one, and from the one to the many". In his view, the universe is to be understood as in process, and not something static. From the rich literature which deals with Whitehead's philosophy I have made a limited selection in order to find thoughts which lie behind the concepts of organic and organism.

An Integrating World View

Bråäkenhielm (in Swedish 1992 p. 28) writes that a philosophical base for an integrating world view can be found in Whitehead's philosophy of process, a world view which implies that reality is bigger and richer than we can measure and weigh using our scientific knowledge, without a strict difference between the physical world, emotional life and the life of the spirit.

Whitehead's scheme is a speculative philosophy (Whitehead 1929, 1978 p. 3) "the endeavour to frame a coherent, logical, necessary system of ideas in terms of which every element of our experience can be interpreted. By this notion of "interpretation" I mean that everything of which we are conscious, as enjoyed, perceived, willed, or thought, shall have the character of a particular instance of the general scheme." In a way, this harmonizes with what Peter Nilsson says, that not only our bodies but also our thoughts have a relation to what originally was formed. Miller's Living Systems also points to the connection between Living Systems and the Universe, and advances a number of hypotheses which need to be tested in order to be confirmed or rejected.

Speculative philosophy is not confined only to illustrating processes of thinking; it also deals which man as a part within a context which is portrayed by "The philosophy of Organism". By "organism" Whitehead generally means a temporally bounded process which organizes a variety of given elements into a new fact" (Lowe 1962 p. 228). Whitehead sees his scheme, as including the living and the nonliving and that it encompasses aesthetic and moral issues. Living Systems is a theory confined to systems, which at the higher levels may consist of organizations, communities, society, and supranational systems. In the next section I will try to point to the thread which runs through his thinking.

THE THREAD

Whitehead writes in (Whitehead 1929. ed. 1978 p. xii):

> "It must be thoroughly understood that the theme of these lectures is not a detached consideration of various traditional philosophical problems which acquire urgency in certain traditional systems of thought. The lectures are intended to state a condensed scheme of cosmological ideas, to develop their meaning by confrontation with the various topics of experience, and finally to elaborate an adequate cosmology in terms of which all particular topics find their interconnections".

and in (Whitehead 1919 p. 3)

> "Nature is that which we observe in perception through the senses. In this sense-perception we are aware of something which is not thought and which is self-contained of thought. This property of being self-contained for thought lies at the base of natural science. It means that nature can be thought of as a closed system whose mutual relations do not require the expression of the fact that they are thought about. Thus in a sense nature is independent of thought."

and (Ford 1984 p. 30)

> "Since nature is that which is perceived, excluding the perceiver, it would seem at first glance that the philosophy of nature should exclude the percipient as well. That, however, just increases the distance between the perceiver and nature. Is nature to be perceived from some absolute, perspectiveless, stance? To be truly perceived, nature must be perceived from a standpoint within nature. But if truly within nature, it would seem to be outside mind. That, precisely, is how Whitehead originally conceived the percipient event: "This is not the mind, that is to say not the percipient. It is that in nature from which the mind perceives". (Whitehead 1920 repr. 1978 p. 107)."

In a similar vein (Miller 1978 p. 1025) writes "I have described and evaluated relevant past theories. In like manner, if a cumulative science of systems is to develop, my theory should be critically taken into account by those who attempt in the future to improve on it and on (p. 1026)

> "The general living systems theory presented in this book is a scientific theory and is therefore less general than a metatheory. It is a specific conceptualization which can be confirmed or disconfirmed by empirical observations. Subjectivists may resist space-time co-ordinates because their private experience is not usually presented to them on such co-ordinates."

Concerning this issue (Lowe 1990 p. 113) writes, "When we make an observation, we perceive something that is not mind. That is, the datum for natural science is not at all mental, for if what is perceived is considered a fact of individual psychology only, no scientific assertions about nature can be tested. Science requires objectivity, that is, that its objects be separate and prior to perception and thought"; and (Lucas 1989 p. 87) states "For Kant, this essential fact was summarized in the dictum that our very possession of certain definite forms of knowledge entails the presupposition of corresponding *a priori* organizing features of mind and consciousness. Whitehead merely adds that reasoned, organized consciousness, in turn, presupposes experience. On this view, Kant's apparent restriction of the notion of experience to the functioning of mental concepts or categories in the production of self-conscious knowledge simply construes the notion of experience too narrowly."

Lucas continues under the heading "The Misappropriation of Kant" (p. 85) "These observations bring us at last to Whitehead's second objection to

Kant, concerning the nature of subjectivity. For Kant, in contrast to Whitehead's interpretation of him, the world does not simply "emerge from the subject". Rather, human subjective experience is constituted by a variety of synthesis of the sensory manifold, of which the synthesis under the Categories of Verstand and issuing in the operational scientific picture of nature constitutes but one. While knowledge or cognition is a central focus of Kantian critiques, such knowledge does not constitute the full range of experience, which is also constituted by important dimensions of Gefühl, or feeling."

SUBJECTIVIST AND OBJECTIVIST POSITION

Whitehead writes that he is endeavouring to establish an objectivist philosophy, capable of bridging the gap between science and that fundamental intuition of mankind which finds its expression in poetry and its practical exemplification in the presuppositions of daily life; he also points out that he is presupposing the organic theory of nature, which he has outlined as a basis for a thoroughgoing objectivism. In the following (Whitehead 1925 p. 88) he describes the difference between a subjectivist and an objectivist position.

> "By a subjectivist basis I mean the belief that the nature of our immediate experience is the outcome of the perceptive peculiarities of the subject enjoying the experience. Thus, though there is a common world of thought associated with our sense perceptions, there is no common world to think about. What we do think about is a common conceptual world applying indifferently to our individual experiences which are strictly personal to ourselves. Such a conceptual world will ultimately find its complete expression in the questions of applied mathematics. There is of course the halfway house of those who believe that our perceptual experience does tell us of a common objective world; but that the things perceived are merely the outcome for us of this world, and are not in themselves elements of the world itself. Also there is the objectivist position. This creed is that the actual elements perceived by our senses are *in themselves* the elements of a common world; and that this world is a complex of things, including indeed our acts of cognition, but transcending them. According to this point of view the things experienced are to be distinguished from our knowledge of them. So far there is dependence, the *things* pave the way for the *cognition*, rather than *vice versa*. But the point is that the actual things experienced enter into a common world which transcends knowledge, though it includes knowledge.

The intermediate subjectivists would hold that the things experienced only indirectly enter into the common world by reason of their dependence on the subject who is cognising. The objectivist holds that the things experienced and the cognisant enter into the common world on equal terms."

Whitehead mentions three reasons to distrust subjectivism:

1. One reason arises from the direct interrogation of our perceptive experience. It appears from this interrogation that we are *within* a world of colours, sounds, and other sense-objects, related in space and time to enduring objects such as stones, trees, and human bodies. We seem to be ourselves elements of this world in the same sense as are the other things which we perceive. But the subjectivist, even the moderate intermediate subjectivist, makes this world, as thus described, dependent on us, in a way which directly traverses our naive experience.
2. My second reason for distrusting subjectivism is based on the particular content of experience. But all these things which it appears certainly happened, are either unknown in detail, or else are reconstructed by inferential evidence. In the face of this content of our personal experience, it is difficult to believe that the experienced is an attribute of our own personality.
3. My third reason is based upon the instinct for action. Just as sense-perception seems to give knowledge of what lies beyond individuality, so action seems to issue in an instinct for self-transcendence. The activity passes beyond self into the known transcendent world. It is activity directed to determinate ends in the known world; and yet it is activity transcending self and it is activity within the known world. It follows therefore that the world, as known, transcends the subject which is cognisant of it. So far as there is dependence, the *things* pave the way for cognition, rather than *vice versa*.

PROCESS AND REALITY

Whitehead (1925 p. 72) writes, "Thus nature is a structure of evolving processes. The reality is the process." In the index to Process and Reality "process" appears nearly 60 times while "reality" does not have a single entry. In (Whitehead 1933) reality is however mentioned several times. On p. 281 we can read "The process is urged onward by operation of the mental pole providing conceptual subject-matter for synthesis with the Reality. There finally emerges the Appearance, which is the transformed Reality after synthesis with the conceptual valuations." Appearance is similar to "sysrep' in Kline (1995 p. 18) where he writes that:

> "The system and the system and the sysrep cannot be the same whenever we are trying to study a piece of the world using a sysrep" "When we are analyzing formal systems, the sysrep is the system of ideas by definition. A sysrep may represent a piece of the real world, but it also may represent a set of ideas. The Appearance is a simplification arising from a process of emphasis and combination. In so far as the Appearance emphasizes connections and qualities of connections which in fact reside in the Reality, then the Appearance is truthful in its relation to Reality."

As a "transcendental corollary" to Kant's view of "Nature" as the end product of the synthesizing activity of the human understanding, Schelling held that nature was in itself a kind of dynamic, creative process or activity culminating in the production of human consciousness." this can be compared to Peter Nilsson's position when he sees that our consciousness is of the same initial matter as the Earth. (Lucas 1989 p. 18) goes on to say "The revolt issuing in the schools of thought collectively termed "process philosophy" specifically condemns: (1) an undynamic concept of materialism; (2) the comfortable and rational, yet distant and stale theological tenants of Deism that seem consequent upon static mechanism and materialism; and most of all (3) the notion of the universe as itself a machine, suggesting, particularly in biology and geology, the relative unimportance and externality of temporal process and flux and the fixed immutability of both organic and inorganic forms."

Chapter 3

SYSTEMS

GENERAL LIVING SYSTEMS

Whitehead held that the primary task of philosophy in the immediate future must be concerned with the ultimate notions, with cosmological schemes of ideas (Leclerc 1961 p. 12). This in order to deal with the issue which (Whitehead 1929 p. 77) points to "The limited morphology of a special science is confessedly incapable of expressing in its own categorical notions all forms which are illustrated in the world. For this reason a cosmology must consider those factors which have not been adequately embraced in some science. It also has to include all the sciences." In the light of present development this seems more and more remote, at the same time as the need for a view which can facilitate co-operation and communication between different areas of science seems more and more necessary. (Whitehead 1919 p. 2) writes "The philosophy of the sciences – conceived as one subject is the endeavour to exhibit all sciences as one science, or – in case of defeat – the disproof of such a possibility." There are differences between science, social science and humanistic science at the level of scientific methodology. These kinds of science do not work with the same prerequisites, and it can therefore be difficult to reach this goal.

At the level of the system Miller maintains that it is desirable to find views in structures and processes which are common to different sciences and by means of exchange achieve advantages of co-ordination. With the help of GLST each subsystem can be treated on the basis of different views of subjects, thereby making it possible to find what may be general.

GLST is a set of related definitions, assumptions, and propositions which deal with reality as an integrated hierarchy of organizations of matter-energy. Miller goes on to say that a general theory of living systems implies a unity of science. He believes that complex structures which carry out living processes can be identified at eight hierarchical levels: cell, organ, organism, group, organization, community, society, and supranational system. I have suggested that a ninth level could be added: the Earth, and also conducted simulation studies at that level. Miller maintains that each level has the same 20 critical subsystems which are essential for life. Some of them process matter or energy and some information and some of them process all three. General Living Systems Theory is in line with (Whitehead 1925 ed. 1967 p. 187) "We cannot think in terms of an indefinite multiplicity of detail; our evidence can acquire its proper importance only if it comes before us marshalled by general ideas." This is also what is declared in (Lowe 1990 p. 110) "Whitehead says, the philosophy he is limiting himself to "is solely engaged in determining the most general conceptions which apply to things observed by the senses. It is not metaphysics, but rather the unified sciences which have nature as their common subject-matter."

In (Whitehead 1919) he says it is "the endeavour to exhibit all sciences as one science". The common purpose of all three works is to replace the philosophic presuppositions of science, and especially the ancient trinity of time, space, and matter which has dominated scientific thinking, with a coherent set of meanings based on relations exhibited in sensory observation. A reorganization of speculative physics is therefore sought in the interconnection of events discriminated in perceptual experience. It is on this score that Whitehead breaks away from the British tradition. His whole project is conceived as an attempt to set out in concrete terms the status of the indispensable concepts needed in physics, but by emphasizing *relatedness* instead of disconnection between independently real and isolated bits of matter in absolute space and time." (Kirk 1993) points to the correspondence of Whitehead's philosophy to Ilya Prigogine's who shows the range from the microscopic to the macroscopic and from the "inanimate" to the biological and the social.

In Chapter 4 (Miller 1978 p. 90) attention is focused on hypotheses which apply to two or more levels of systems, because of their powerful generality. These are more than propositions of systems theory: they are *general* systems theoretical hypotheses" and he continues on p. 114 "They demand the most careful and rigorous conceptualization and research design. They require the skills of several disciplines. But their findings are important, crucial in the development of general theory about living systems. Such investigations can best be conducted in interdisciplinary research institutes, centres, and groups." On p. 85 he declares, in a statement which is in line with Whitehead's thinking: "There are undoubtedly many similarities and possibly many cross-level identities in the phenomena of life. There are also significant differences among the various levels, types, and individuals in the gamut of living systems, as well as in the ways different scientific disciplines investigate them. Before us lies a search for pattern in individuality, for unity in diversity."

ABSTRACTED SYSTEMS

Units

The units of *abstracted systems* are relationships abstracted or selected by an observer in the light of his interests, theoretical viewpoint, or philosophical bias. Some relationships may be empirically determinable by some operation carried out by the observer, but others are not, being only his concepts.

Relationships

The relationships mentioned above are observed to inhere and interact in concrete, usually living systems. Since abstracted systems are usually oriented toward relationships rather than toward the concrete systems which have those relationships, spatial arrangements are not usually emphasized. Consequently their physical limits often do not coincide spatially with the boundaries of any concrete system, although they may.

Abstracted Versus Concrete Systems

One fundamental distinction between abstracted and concrete systems is that the boundaries of abstracted systems may at times be conceptually established at regions which cut through the units and relationships in the physical space occupied by concrete systems.

Abstracted Versus Conceptual Systems

The two kinds of systems differ in that some units and/or relationships of every abstracted system are empirically determined and this is not true of any conceptual system.

Processes

Miller also held a standpoint in living systems which says that all change over time of matter-energy or information in a system is process. (Miller 1978 p. 30) "A subsystem, thus, is identified by the process it carries out. It exists in one or more identifiable structural units of the system. These specific, local, distinguishable structural units are called components or members or parts." Since living systems aims at empirical verification, the concept of process is studied in relation to components or parts in a structure/scheme according to the definitions given below.

Conclusion

This chapter confines itself to examining the relations/links between Whitehead's philosophy and Living Systems, using quotations from Whitehead and literature which deals with Whitehead's philosophy. As a result I have shown how Miller is inspired by Whitehead's process philosophy, and how this laid a foundation for GLST. By studying the philosophy behind GLST the difference between Living Systems theory and other kinds of systems thinking can be more easily understood. There is a line from Whitehead to Living systems and from there to the application of Living Systems which will be shown in Chapter 12 Application and Simulation. If Whitehead takes a clear stand for an objectivist view then Michael Jackson, as is shown in the next chapter, takes a stand for a subjectivist view which can be related to the philosopher Immanuel Kant to whom Michael Jackson refers.

Chapter 4

ALTERNATIVE VIEWS OF SYSTEMS

INTRODUCTION

I have briefly tried to depict how Whitehead saw the difference between objectivity and subjectivity, and indicated that he took stand for an objectivist view. Behind different "management solving problems" as described by Michael Jackson there seems to be a dividing line between objectivism and subjectivism which leads to different kinds of systems thinking. I intend to make comparisons between the content and application of these two alternatives, on the basis of the grid *Figure 1* which Jackson has presented in (Jackson 1995 a).

He writes on (p. 30) "The grid introduced as Figure 1 helps to demonstrate the relationship between the various approaches and makes it possible to understand that they do not necessarily clash with each other" In a corresponding Figure 1 in (Jackson 1995 p. 26) there is a question-mark placed in the lower right-hand corner which is intended to show "the result of combining the axes in an ideal-type grid in which problem contexts can be seen as becoming more difficult to manage as you get increasing divergence of values and interests, as you get increasing complexity". Jackson's intention is by means of these figures, to point up differences between different kinds of systems thinking; his interpretation seems to be based on Figure 2.2 in (Flood and Jackson 1991 p. 32). In my opinion these two figure*s* are an over-simplification regarding the differences between the approaches (according to the figure), and I will in the following indicate points of view regarding the content of the axes.

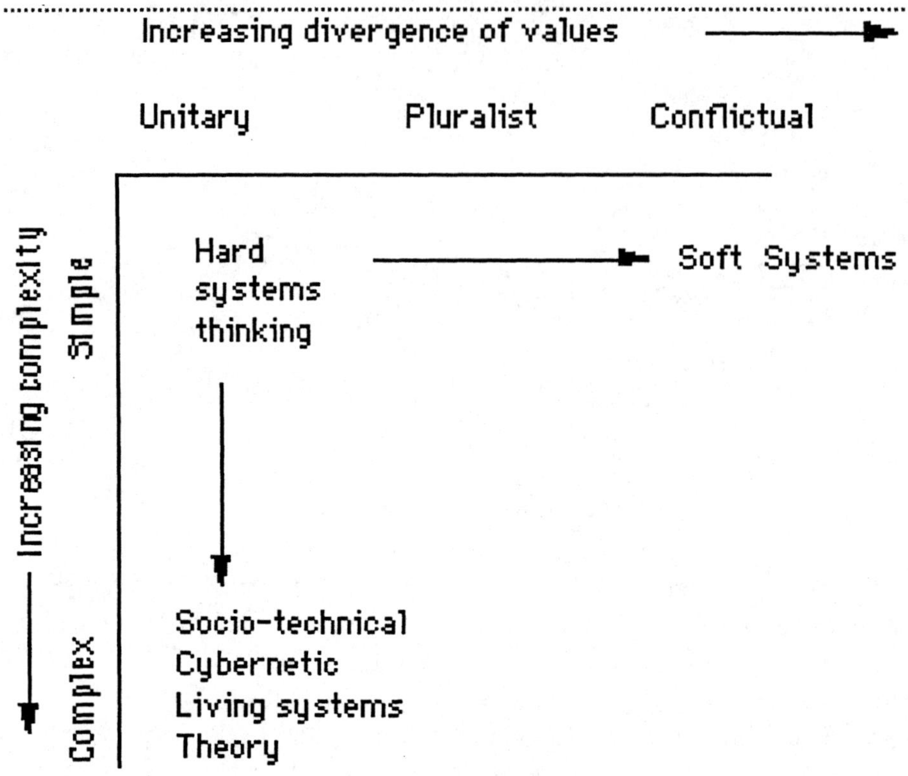

Figure 4:1 is taken from (Jackson 1996 c)

SYSTEMS IN LIVING SYSTEMS

Whitehead (1978 p. 148) writes "You cannot cling to the idea that we have two sets of experiences of nature, one of primary qualities which belong to the objects perceived, and one of secondary qualities which are the products of our mental excitements. All we know of nature is in the same boat, to sink or to swim together". According to Whitehead we can decide whether to proceed on an objectivist or a subjectivist basis. He chooses to proceed on an objectivist basis. What we observe is what we observe. "Awareness must be confined to awareness in relation to body."

Living Systems declares its chief purpose as being "to state in prose a conceptual system concerning variables – units and relationships – which have important formal identities or isomorphisms to concrete, living systems." Living Systems distinguishes between three kinds of systems, which are given in Miller (1978 p. 17-19):

- Conceptual system. Units of a conceptual system are terms, such as words, numbers or other symbols including those in computer simulations and programs.
- A concrete system, real, or veridical system is a non-random accumulation of matter-energy, in a region in physical space-time, which is organized into interacting interrelated subsystems or components.
- Abstracted system. Units. The units of *abstracted systems* are relationships abstracted or selected by an observer in the light of his interests, theoretical viewpoint, or philosophical bias.

Miller uses the words organism and organic in the same meaning as Whitehead, not only in a biological sense but also to point at an ability to organize i.e. to refer to a society or an organization in a similar way as is quoted above from Lynn Margulis and Dorion Sagan (Margulis, Sagan 1995 p. 177) "Nor did life stop at complex cells and multicellular beings. It went on, forging societies and communities and the living biosphere itself."

Living Systems – The Vertical Axis

I would maintain that Living Systems gives better possibilities for expressing pluralistic thoughts in a more fruitful way than when representatives of different subject areas depict society as a social, economic or some other subject- oriented system, without the kind of common ground, which in Living Systems, is related to conditions for the survival of the system. The choice of a common ground for discussion, living systems, is made among other things after a critical study of the alternatives to systems thinking which have been shown in Lane and Jackson (1995 pp. 217-228) and in (Frandberg 1994).

Jackson notes, (Jackson a, p. 27), that when objectives were relatively clear they – systems analyses and systems engineering – rested upon an assumption which was categorized, according to Figure 1, as unitary. They relied here upon there being a shared, and therefore readily identifiable, objective. This depends on how one sees objective. There are perhaps goals/objectives which are readily identifiable but not shared between individuals or between individuals and the group, or between the citizens and the state. There are also objectives which are shared but not readily identifiable. Unitary systems thinking then begins to suffer from a lack of clear definition. In this case the objective is however the "ultimate objective" – to study the conditions for the survival of the living system – and does not belong to the vertical axis of unitary thinking. In this connection I notice that Jackson in (Lane and Jackson 1995 p. 220), has written that LST is currently the most productive area of research in GST.

I agree with Jackson in his view on system dynamics (SD) with regard to simulations carried out before a theory has been declared on the presupposition of causal relationships in extensive models. The number of causal relationships are infinite. Against the background of the discussion above I am aware of what

Whitehead has written in (Whitehead 1929 p. 75):

> "Up to a point a scheme is invaluable. It clarifies thought, it suggests observation, it explains fact. But there is a strict limit to the utility of any finite scheme. If it the scheme be pressed beyond its proper scope, definite error results. The art of the speculative Reason consists quite as much in the transcendence of schemes as in their utilization."

This course of action studies changes in every subsystem on the basis, for example, of statistical records, without any advance presumption of causal relationships. The results of simulations are seen as variations which can point to covariations which may subsequently examine the validity of the theory. Peter Corning writes in (Systems Research and Behavioral Science Vol. 15 Number 6 1998 Nov.-Dec. p. 455). In order to understand a complex multi-level system at least three complementary analyses are necessary, namely: (1) a reductionist study of the detailed structure and function of the 'parts' at various levels, (2) a systemic view of the 'whole' and its emergent properties (including its behavior), and (3) an understanding of how the parts (and levels) fit together and interact with one another.

Complexity – The Vertical Axis

Beyond a certain limit it does not become meaningful to talk about increasing complexity. When can it be confirmed that one problem is more complex than another? At what point is one required to change methods or points of view as the complexity continually grows? Complexity increases along both axes. If unitary systems thinking is developed to take account of continually increasing complexity, then it can no longer reasonably be called "unitary". Nicolis and Prigogine (1989 p. 8), write that: "when compared with the difference between physic-chemical and biological phenomena the difference between simple and complex is not so sharp as we intuitively assume."

Is there a difference in the way the increasing complexity along the horizontal axis (pluralist conflictual) is to be understood and the increasing complexity along the vertical axis (the unitary) John Briggs and F. David Peat write in (Briggs and Peat p. 147) "The idea of simplicity is falling apart. Any direction you go in there's complexity"; and on (p. 127) "On one side, a simple regular system reveals its implicit complexity. On the other, complexity reveals its implicit coherence"; and, finally, on (p. 43)

> "In fact, the orbital situation we have just discussed provides our first glimpse into a new realization spreading across science – that randomness is interleaved with order, that simplicity enfolds complexity, complexity harbours simplicity, and that order and chaos can be repeated at smaller and smaller scales– a phenomenon the scientists of chaos have dubbed 'fractal'".

Systems thinking has been said to be the science of complexity, but in an article by John Horgan in (Scientific American, June 1995, p. 74), "From Complexity to Perplexity", The author gives, after providing some examples, doubts about its possibility of success.

Cybernetics – The Vertical Axis

Cybernetics is presented in (Figure 1, Jackson 1996 c) as belonging along the vertical axis, "unitary thinking". Cybernetics ought also to be well suited for examining if one has been sufficiently creative or critical, and would in this case equally belong to the horizontal axis. Cybernetics is integrated in systems thinking and belongs as an important part in the theory of living systems, where steady states in all living systems are controlled by feedback. Total Systems Intervention (TSI) in Robert L. Flood and Michael Jackson (1991) depicts a feedback loop between creative phase, choice phase, and implementation. This seems to presume that creativity and choice result in an implementation which is in accordance with a desired result. When the implementation is made: does one then know where one stands in relation to objectives, efficiency and effectiveness, or organization etc. over time? How does one know when creativity has been such that one has moved further in the direction of choice? Are not creativity and critical thinking connected in such a way that one cannot think creatively without simultaneously thinking critically?

The idea of defining creative and critical thinking as a feedback process seems to be all too limited in relation to the whole network of information and experiences which influences our actions. The relation between observer and observed system has for example been studied by second order cybernetics. Stuart Umpleby writes in (Umpleby 1994 p. 2) that the "second order cyberneticians" claim that knowledge is a biological phenomenon (Maturana 1970), that each individual constructs his or her own "reality" (von Foerster, 1973) and that knowledge "fits" but does not match the world of experience (von Glasersfeld, 1987)"

INNATE SUBJECTIVITY

In (Flood and Jackson 1991 p. 79) it is written that "SD simply does not deal with the innate subjectivity of human beings and the consequences of this for the study of social systems." This thinking seems to be in line with what Umpleby says in (Umpleby 1994 p. 10), that in soft systems thinking "the inner world has primacy over the outer world, action is based on philosophical position, and the free realm of ideas is preferred over the necessary realm of matter. In all it displays a high regard for philosophical thought. In Kant's idealism the a priori is rational form and the a posteriori is empirical matter. In other words, a person composes a conception of the world and then acts on that idea."

Jackson uses the word rational and refers to Kant's philosophy as a critical philosophy in contrast to a dogmatic one. Dogmatic denotes every line of thought which starts from certain aspects without carefully presenting them and examining their claims to validity. Criticism, or critical philosophy, pays attention to this task; – in this case the importance of thinking creatively and critically (with explicit emphasis on critical) and then making implementations. Considerable importance in this regard is accorded to how mind works. When mind is chosen as a foundation for representing images of reality, it is of decisive consequence how mind functions. How and when do I know when I am creative enough to create alternatives and when I am critical enough to make an appropriate choice in order in relation to the objective which I aim at. The result of the implementation will be related to my personal ability and the result will be judged in relation to the individual person "if subjectivity is to be made central "as in the following quotation from (Jackson 1995 a p. 28)

> "Along this dimension, the breakthrough came when the aim of producing one single, objective model of a problem situation was abandoned. This was seen to be both impossible and undesirable given multiple values and interests. The trick was to make subjectivity central in the methodological process and to work with a variety of models of the world".

I too realize that it can not always be fruitful to work with a single model of the world. But after a theory is chosen (in my case living systems) it does not exclude that other alternatives may be chosen in the way Jackson points out (in Jackson a p. 30): "I have tried to develop a meta-methodology, creative problem-solving, which shows how to work with different methodologies in a complementary fashion – an approach which we are seeking all the time to improve."

We always carry on a dialogue as to consider what is creative and critical. This is not anything which especially characterizes soft systems thinking or TSI. In all situations it is a condition that we think both critically and creatively otherwise we would be immobilised. Even if one has been thinking creatively and critically an observer outside or inside the organization can still say that it was not creative and critical enough. The argument against a choice other than systems thinking according to for example TSI seems to be that other alternatives – such as Living Systems – are not creative and critical.

Soft Systems – The Horizontal Axis

Jackson mentions influences from religion and politics, which in my view do not belong in this context, and writes in (Lane & Jackson 1995 p. 244) "Critical systems thinking is a politically conscious and self-reflective approach" ... "liberating people from dominance by other people and forces they do not control". In (Jackson 1995 a p. 39) we can read that "Kant's pre-eminent concern was man's release from domination by Church dogma. He wanted people to think freely for themselves and not to be slaves of what the Church told them to think "

What Kant seems to mean is that if people had had the opportunity to think freely, they perhaps would have found a way which had allowed them to think freely and distinguish between true or false and good or bad. The thoughts of Luhman, Focoult and Derrida, who are quoted in (Jackson 1996 a p. 40), "The idea of people escaping from self-incurred tutelage to think freely and decide for themselves is a con "have all too often been proven right."

How and when will increasingly different values in a conflictual behaviour situation result in a plan of action? Could the plan of action instead be attained by means of consensus? Both consensus and conflict presuppose democracy but is there always democracy which allows people to think freely in an organization or in a society? Man is a social being who is involved in a social context from which she/he cannot free her/himself.

Divergence of Values – The Horizontal Axis

Is an increasing complexity along the horizontal axis easier to understand in a better way because it is seen in the light of an increasing divergence of values from unitary to pluralist and conflictual? If there is a continually increasing divergence of values can a decision then ever be made? When does one know when it is appropriate to take a decision? Values lies deep in human beings and one is not always aware of how they have come about and what causes changes in them. Am I always aware what lies behind my choice of values, which over time determine what is true or false or good or bad and thus the choices we make?

Cohen writes (Cohen 1968 p. 126) "If social systems are systems of interaction then change must result – usually without intention – from the conditions and processes of interaction itself." This interaction can, put simply, be seen from two points of view: one when consensus, and one when conflict in a dialectical process is predominant. The class struggle is one example of the latter. There are examples where sharply increasing divergence of values lie behind the disintegration of societies.

TSI – THE HORIZONTAL AXIS

I would like to start with a quotation from Flood and Jackson (1991 p. 244) "What should we do as managers, planners, decision makers or consultants when all the evidence we have highlights coercive forces at work?" When one aims, as does Jackson according to the title of his paper at the ISSS meeting, to cope with world problems difficulties are bound to be encountered, since there are so many problems of different kinds and at different levels over time.

Even if Jackson does not mean problem as I assume in *Figure 5* but problems in general, still in many cases problems and their connections will appear. This question is treated in Flood and Jackson (1991) by showing the Viable System Model of Stafford Beer. It has also been dealt with under the headline "TSI in action" in Flood and Jackson (1991 chapter 10.2) and shown in (Jackson 1996 b). In this connection it is interesting to notice that Ulrich in (Ulrich 1983 p. 371) writes, where he reflects on the sources of deception in the cybernetics tools they (Stafford Beer and the Allende Government) employed: "As long as these tools are understood as scientific and value-neutral, it will be deceptive to expect any significant contribution to social and democratic progress from them".

PROBLEM DESCRIPTION

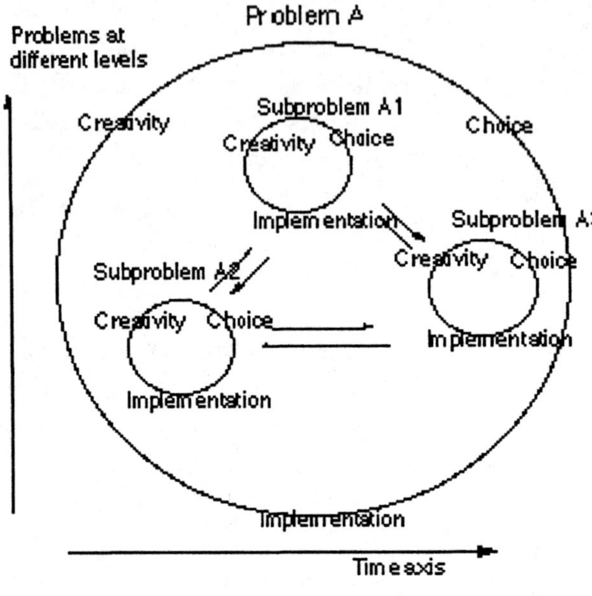

Figure 4:2 Within every Problem A may lie problems at different levels, for example at level 5, 4, 3, and 1a-1d according to VSM) and in different chronological order.

The larger circle is here supposed to illustrate the importance of co-ordinating problems, not least when coercive forces are dealt with. When living systems is used it facilitates thinking creatively and critically. Neither is there any obstacle which prevents LS from studying such suggestions as are assumed to depend on "coercive forces at work", (when and if it is possible to identify them). It is the result of the suggestions as such which is the object of study in living systems, irrespective of whether they are politically, religiously or otherwise motivated. But as Peter Corning in (Corning 1996 pp. 675-676) under "Synergy and the Systems Sciences" emphasizes, "Synergy – the combined effects produced by two (or more) parts, elements or individuals – is a ubiquitous phenomenon in nature and human societies alike". This alternative seems to be more in line with living systems, which presumes the existence of subsystems acting in order to maintain the survival of living systems.

A Suggestion to Combine the Points of View Along the Axes

Fritiof Capra (1996 p. 267) refers to Humberto Maturana and Fransisco Varela, and writes that living systems are cognitive systems and that living systems is a process of cognition. He goes on to write:

> "Cognition, then, is not a representation of an independently existing world, but rather a continual *bringing forth of a world* through the process of living. The interactions of a living system with its environment are cognitive interactions, and the process of living itself is a process of cognition"

Living systems seems to be well in line with these thoughts. Man is a part of this network of processes, relations and structures which the living system forms. In this network there is no boundary between different kinds of networks. The partitioning along two axes in *Figure 1*, as I understand founded on the matrix in *Figure 2.2* in (Flood and Jackson 1991), does not reflect the immense number of networks of processes and structures within systems thinking.

Flood and Jackson write in (Flood and Jackson p. 79) that systems cannot be studied, using the objective, from-the–outside approach of systems dynamics. On (p. 244) they talk as is mentioned above about liberating people from dominance by other people and forces they do not control and in a later passage about the innate subjectivity of human beings and the consequences of this for the study of social systems. Capra sees in (Capra 1996 p. 296) the danger of splitting up society by means of abstract thinking:

> The power of abstract thinking has led us to treat the natural environment – the web of life – as if it consisted of separate parts to be exploited by different interest groups. Moreover we have extended this fragmented view to our human society, dividing it into different nations, races, religious and political groups. The belief that all these fragments – in ourselves, in our environment, and in our society – are really separate has alienated us from nature and from our fellow human beings and thus diminished us. To regain our full humanity, we have to regain our experience of connectedness with the entire web of life.

CONCLUSION

Living systems, when it uses abstracted systems, does have similarities with soft systems thinking, although they start from different points of view concerning the relationships between the innate and the outer world. The above points out that GLST is closer to an application of systems thinking than approaches founded on a philosophical conviction that reality is always mainly interpreted on the basis of individual qualifications.

There are people who take a stand which can be said to be situated between the objectivist and the subjectivist view; they see themselves as soft objectivists. Our knowledge is not a complete mirror of either the object (as hard objectivism maintains) or the subjectivism (as hard subjectivism maintains). Because our knowledge, or our interpretations, change – although only to a certain extent – over the course of history it seems to be evident that our knowledge has both subjective and objective elements. This means that we have a tendency to transfer subjective elements to our pictures and then believe that they are objective. Living systems sees reality as an unfolding process from the cell to the Earth in much the same way as is expressed in Margulis and Sagan (1995) and in Capra (1996). The most fruitful role for philosophy is perhaps in increasing the understanding of different points of view on man's relation to the process of life.

In the discussion above about different views on and aspects of designing models where I have pointed to the importance of anchoring the models to a theory. It is also important that the models can serve as a basis for discussion about the models relation to reality. In the next chapter I want to discuss qualities of models of society and how they can be implemented.

Chapter 5

VIEWS OF SOCIETY AND SYSTEMS

CONNECTEDNESS OF PROBLEMS IN HUMAN SOCIETY

One early report "The Town as a System" Frandberg (1982) was aimed to produce a computerized model in an initial attempt to describe structures and processes in living systems. It contained no more than five subsystems. The connection between subsystems was described using the program language Dynamo. The paper stressed the importance, as is suggested by Bateson (1979) of looking at society with the help of systems theory, cybernetics, holistic medicine, ecology, and the theory of form and psychology. It also referred to Stafford Beer (1973) who, through his example of the esoteric box, showed that the community appears to be unable to develop a metastructure which would permit co-operation in the solution of the community problems that demand general knowledge and an overall view, and that this can result in a society that is fragile and difficult to understand. The paper cited works by Sir Geoffrey Vickers, George H. von Wright, Robert Vacca and De Greene who pointed to the need for flow-directed models which study changes rather than static structures.

It was a first attempt from my own point of view to describe reality in terms of GLST, and was intended to provide an alternative to the kinds of studies of society to which Miller refers (p. 893): "Matter-energy processing by societies has been underemphasized. Quantification has been infrequent." This "underemphasizing" of matter-energy processing has been a contributory cause of the fact that, for example, environmental problems were not noticed in time. It then seemed important to justify and assemble the arguments for my choice of GLST, and it was important to work out and present a comparison with different theories of society.

It was therefore in report “nr 2” “Connectedness of Problems in Human Society” I made a comparison with different viewpoints collected from Beer (1979), Churchman (1982) and Campbell (1981). Over and above the comparisons in “nr 2” a comparison is made here between the views of Werner Ulrich and GLST. Ulrich is chosen because he seems to represent an overall critical attitude towards General Systems Theory. Ulrich’s views resemble in many aspects those of C. West Churchman and Peter Checkland. This may be of interest since he writes that his study partly goes against the objectivistic understanding of “rational” planning in contemporary systems science. He exemplifies these Ulrich (1983 p. 20) “with the concept of systems with predominantly technocratic approaches to planning such as RAND-systems analysis, systems engineering, social cybernetics, General Systems Theory (which is neither general nor theoretical) and several others” Ulrich makes no comment or direct reference concerning GLST.

Ulrich is of the opinion that “the free citizen” knows what “social reality ought to be like”. Social reality touches also on questions such as emotions, relations to other people, cultural activities, all of which are difficult to describe and answer with philosophy and science. How is one to answer these questions? What is a “free citizen”? Is there anyone who is not more or less ‘caught’ in his own conception of the world ? A world that over the years has been shaped by external and internal forces. Can the individual know what “social reality” would have been like if these factors had been different? Does the “free citizen” in an ever-changing world know what social reality ought to be like?

A few pages earlier Ulrich analyses the difference between H. A. Simon’s and C. West Churchman’s view of systems, where Simon represents an “analytic-reductionist tradition” and Churchman “the nonobjectivist and antireductionist tradition” where subjectivity must be included in the definition of objectivity. A designer cannot free herself /himself of value judgements when designing “purposeful systems” see *Figure 5:1*. Ulrich describes a way to attain the last-named goal, namely (p. 336) to “ask for the degree of purposefulness as it is revealed by the system’s design, not by its designer’s intentions or claims.” The last sentence expresses a difference between what is subjectively wished and the wish in the form of a collective. How does the wish of an individual as it is expressed in what society ought to be like relate to the system's design? This is a question that is and has been much discussed. It is not enough to know what social reality ought to be like. One must also be in a position to influence the situation so that one reaches that reality. This can be done in a number of ways, but the way indicated by Ulrich is through a system that rests on a philosophical basis and does not leave the realms of philosophy. One flaw in *Figure 5:1* Ulrich (1983), which describes the course of events that lead to rational planning, is that it has no time axis. This means that the figure describes a static state of affairs. *Figure 5:1* is based on six different "subsystems" and is of a complexity that is far removed from what can be communicated to people who do not operate on the philosophical plane. The table starts with "Root metaphor: Social group (polis) rather than machine or organism and continues with Systems paradigm "Purposeful Systems", Guiding questions, Is a system S designed to become a purposeful social system?, Taxonomy of problem-solving dimensions, Anatomy of purposefulness, Actual Mapping ("Is") and Ideal mapping ("Ought"), Process of unfolding (Practical discourse) in order to attain "Rational" planning via Systems rationality vs Social rationality.

For one thing, the time axis should be included when it is a question of the time difference between the first and the final step in the planning process and, for another, it should be related in some way to the changes that take place over time in the reality the planning is concerned with. In certain cases considerable time will elapse before the planning process is completed (in fact the process may take so long that the reality has had time to change so much that it no longer corresponds to the reality on which the planning was based). It is difficult to believe that all the phases of a planning process can take place at the same time and that the process is always in step with a changing reality. Do the gains expressed in terms of care of the environment, material welfare and quality of life correspond to what is achieved if one plans along these lines?

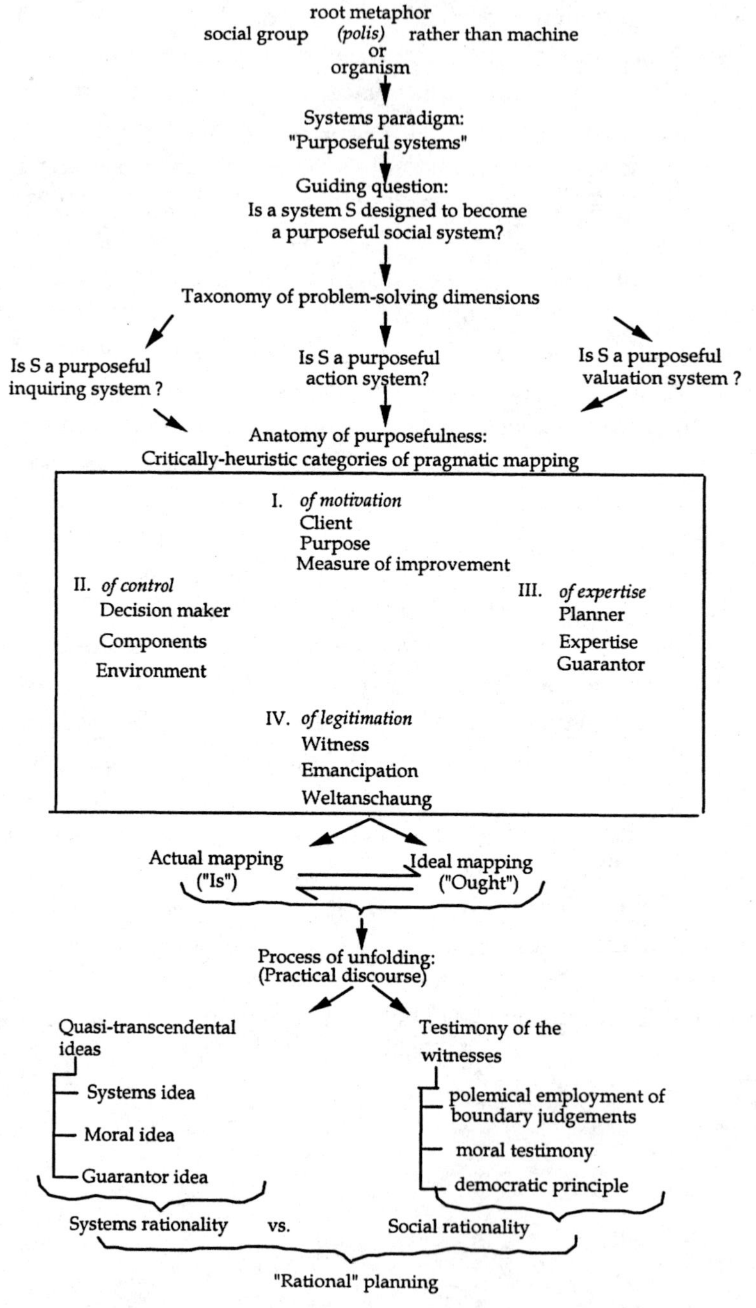

Figure 5:1 Is taken from Ulrich 1983 (p. 342). It shows, starting from "root metaphor", how "rational planning" is achieved.

How are we to record the sacrifices and gains? Ulrich (1983 p. 20) writes that his point of view is a philosophical one:

> "Critical Systems Heuristics will provide planners and concerned citizens alike with an effective tool of reflection and criticism-reflection on the inevitable normative content of all planning. Planning is rational, from the perspective of this study, if the involved planners and the affected citizens make clear to themselves and to each other this normative content."

Gustavsson (1988) has, starting from a comparison between different views of man, society and nature, discussed what is possible to analyse and what is possible to foresee. Different world views and different ideologies compete with each other. They must therefore be studied side by side, compared and critically scrutinized, in order to see what may lead to new kinds of oppression and what can lead to human dignity, liberation within society and another relation to nature. When one however assumes as Prigogine, does that order arises from chaos, a non-equilibrium (active, hot, and energetic — a turbulent chaos far removed from equilibrium) where new qualities continuously arise, one can question if the world is any longer possible to foresee. In Briggs (1990) in the Chapter "Times Arrow" (p. 143) the problem is posed thus: "at its bifurcation points, the system undergoing flux is, in effect, offered a "choice" of orders. The internal feedback of some of the choices is so complex that there is a virtual infinity of degrees of freedom. *Figures 9:4, 9:5,* and *9:6* show the complexity of the feedback processes. Systems thinking and the theory of living systems, as an approach to dealing with complexity, does not treat the problem within a deterministic view. Systems thinking and the theory of living systems is a way, to critically analyse and synthesize our living conditions taking as a point of departure the conditions for our survival. It may be an attempt to answer the question between what "is" and "ought", to be in *Figure 5:1.*

One is reminded of what is said in Bernstein (1976) where it is described how those who at the end of the 1950 s and in the beginning of the 1960 s placed their hope in a rebirth of a critical theory which could unite theory and practice were disappointed, since critical theory failed to provide any strategic orientation in what was to be done. He subsequently emphasizes that we are never in a position to know with absolute certainty that critical enlightenment has been effective — that it has liberated us from ideologically frozen constraints of the past, and initiated genuine self-reflection. Bernstein questions the sharp distinction between "the hard natural sciences" and what Habermas calls the historical-hermeneutical disciplines. He maintains that the process which is to be found according to in critical theory also takes place within empirical-analytic-sciences, for at their very foundation they require interpretative principles and a rational resolution of the conflict of interpretations.

As was noted earlier, science cannot be viewed as independent of philosophy. Living Systems does not disregard philosophy; philosophy does not disregard values and therefore does not disregard the approach Ulrich describes in Ulrich (1983) the following sentence (p. 25) as: "self-reflective, that is to say, philosophical rather than scientific. In the domain of social inquiry and design, it is irrelevant if not deceptive to be scientific without being openly and critically philosophical." However, in view of the different schools of philosophy it is unlikely that this point will be resolved because one cannot determine which kind of planning contains an explanatory "normative content" and what this means where planning is concerned. Ulrich takes up a discussion about the concept of normative content when he brings up the question as to how we can avoid falling prey to the objectivist illusion when we neither logically nor empirically can establish the validity in a question. In the following quotation Ulrich (1983 p. 198) refers:

> "Normative content, i.e. their inevitable value premises and, in the context of application, their normative implications. Normative presuppositions, just like metaphysical ones, cannot be validated either logically or empirically (in terms of empirical-analytic science); neither what is logically consistent nor what is empirically given can tell us what ought to be."

He also asks how we may distinguish the metaphysical and the normative content. The above sentence can be interpreted as saying that what I have experienced and have an understanding of in quantitative and qualitative terms cannot be used in a planning situation where attempts are being made to determine what "ought to be." How this experience can be linked with philosophy is one of the big questions posed throughout history. Can we say that what *Figure 5:1* corresponds to the demands set out in the preceding sentence?

Figure 5:1 does not take up the question of how feedback takes place between the first step "the root metaphor" and the final one "Rational planning" in the planning process. Nor does it present points of view on how the process can take place between the different steps. This means that there is no discussion of the question of how the communication process takes place, for example, in regard to the transmission capacity of the different information channels or the information processing capacity of the different receivers and transmitters. Can the sacrifices and gains be placed in such a relation to each other as to encourage a "free citizen" to go along with the process in *Figure 5:1*. The gain can, for example, be expressed as the difference between an improved quality of life and, say, the cost of measures to improve the environment or of closing down production plants that are dangerous to health, compared with an improved state of health. As matters stand today we are increasingly forced to pay heed to the conditions for survival. This means that we must find out what is important and then choose the right combination of measures that will yield the best conditions.

Johannisson (1988) has presented a vivid description of how differences of opinion over hundreds of years have prevailed between those who wanted to measure human qualities and put a price expressed in quantitative terms on the human being, and those who felt that the worth of the human being and the nation lay in the skill and morality that the individual person represented. She takes as an example how those involved in road traffic planning are still making a comparison between the cost of the loss of human lives and the cost of implementing measures to make road traffic safer. Such a weighing up of pros and cons is more difficult if, in a pluralistic society, we cannot see the connections and differences and exchange opinions about what society looks like and the conditions that apply as regards the growth of plants and animals and how these interact in the biosphere.

In his preface Mumford (1938) gives an example of the second opinion when he writes that his intention has been to examine in a more unified way an area that has hitherto been dealt with by specialists working along separate lines, and with a view to social activity present the fundamental principles according to which the renewal of our human surroundings — buildings, dwellings, cities, regions — can take place. Mumford seeks wholeness. This is lost when specialists develop viewpoints and methods with the help of which a society is created that pays no heed to the survival of the individual and the society. His approach points to the ultimate objective, namely, that the most important needs from the point of view of life fulfilment are those which generate spiritual activity and promote spiritual growth: the need for order, continuity, meaning, value, aim and purpose. His description of what basically is important for a society (a city) is therefore different from the approach adopted in Forrester (1969) who sees industry, inhabitants and housing as the fundamental activities.

As was pointed out earlier, an application of GLST would promote a dialogue between individuals and those representing different social interests. After all, a dialogue between these would enable concrete descriptions to be made of the different alternatives, and it would be unfortunate if this is dismissed on the grounds put forward by Peter Checkland, who maintains that it represents a method that is suitable only for dictators, demagogues and determinists.

It is possible to discern a parallel to Churchman (1982) who talks about the difference between Thought and Wisdom, or the difference that Ulrich notes between "practical reason", which "can tell us how to use our freedom of choice so as to realize better human (social) systems", and "theoretical reason", which "can give us insight into causal laws and the evolutionary process of natural systems." Ulrich (1983 p. 220) "reason is theoretical if it secures critical understanding of what is; it is practical if it secures critical understanding of what ought to be." The way to what Ulrich regards as practical reason will be difficult to communicate and transfer to "Rational" planning which would be comparable to an "immediate method of action", which is what Whitehead means by practical reason. Whitehead (1929 p. 11) distinguishes "between the theorctical Reason as seeking a complete understanding and the practical Reason as seeking an immediate method of action."

There is no disputing the fact that an approach to the design and assessment of systems is desirable. Ulrich, however, limits himself to describing purposeful systems and in so doing he sets a strict limit to what he regards as systems. Ulrich's definition (p. 334) is:

> "We designate a system S as a purposeful system if S is self-reflective with respect to its own normative implications, seen from the point of view not only of the involved but also of the affected, and if S has at least partial autonomy in determining its client, its purposes etc. "Partial autonomy" precludes the possibility that a system is purely extrinsically motivated; it means that a system can exercise its own will in choosing its goals."

The definition and its subsequent implications have their origin in man's endeavour formulated long ago by the Greeks — "know thyself". Over the centuries it has been a dream that man can exercise its own will in choosing its goals. We are now faced with the question of what enables mankind to exercise his own will. It is enough in this connection to refer to the differences of opinion shown to have existed over the years in the dialogue between those who represent the view that man has free will and those who hold the opposite view. Ulrich maintains that the categories which a heuristic approach might yield cannot of course be justified theoretically (i.e. by demonstrating their necessity) but only heuristically, i.e. by referring to their empirically contingent usefulness. To find empirically contingent usefulness that the categories of a heuristic approach might yield would require one to describe reality in some way, and the problem is that describing reality is far from easy, since the description of reality made by a person may vary considerably over the years and even from day to day. His aim is to clarify properties so that they can be more easily observed and communicated. Ulrich maintains (p. 334) that Ackoff and Emery (1972) seek

> "to define the concepts of function, goal seeking, and purpose with all the rigor of the [causal-mechanistic] concepts used in the physical sciences" and As rigorous as their conceptualization of purposeful systems is, its predominantly behavioristic and frequently mathematical language offers little help to the planner in dealing with the problem of practical reason."

Concerning theories (According to Campbell these "theories" could almost be described as philosophy) Campbell (1981) has in part two chosen the following examples of "theories" which have been put forward in the aim of describing the human society:

Aristotle:	The Civic Community
Thomas Hobbes:	Instrumental Individualism
Adam Smith:	The Social System
Karl Marx:	A Conflict Theory
Emil Durkheim:	A Consensus Theory
Max Weber:	An Action Theory
Alfred Schultz:	A Phenomenological Approach

As is noted above, one of the difficulties where these "theories" are concerned is to know at what point the accumulation of empirical evidence counts decisively against the basic postulates of a theory or, in other words, when experience does not fit into Ulrich's model, according to which it should lead to rational planning. It is not possible to assume that people who take part in the process are uninfluenced by different theories concerning how the connection between theory and empiricism is to be interpreted.

Campbell made use of a similar method in order to describe society and came to a similar conclusion. It is according to Campbell an over-simplification to class a theory of society as individualistic or holistic, positivist or interpretatavist, functional or active. Such theories cannot be easily classified in compartments labelled conflict or consensus, materialist or idealist, descriptive or normative. They are more complex than that. Campbell ends by taking up three recurring philosophical questions which have a bearing on the choice between competing approaches namely:

(1) free will versus determinism
(2) the nature of explanation and
(3) the objectivity of value judgements.

Perhaps the most intractable tension is that between verifiability and intelligibility. The pursuit of "objective" in the sense of observable scientific data is the constant obsession of those social theorists who long for the certainty and intellectual respectability attaching to the natural sciences. Miller touches on these issues when he says in Miller (1978) (p. 1049):

> "Basic living systems theory and research do not, at first glance, seem to have much relevance to such important human problems as war, economic cycles, racial differences, civil rights legislation, improved education, the population explosion, or the energy crisis. As a result, many people try to solve these problems directly, without reference to a basic conceptual system."

Trying to apply a strictly rational decision model that requires perfect knowledge of the complete set of alternatives in a decision situation, as well as the outcomes to be expected from each, at the level of society is even more difficult than at the levels of organism, group, and organization. He also points to the difficulties of connecting decisions with their outcomes over time, and says that there is no perfectly rational solution to most administrative problems. He continues:

"Estimation of the comparative costs of the different alternatives is a formidable job also because of the variety of units in which they are assessed, including long-term loss of confidence in decider components by components of the system, erosion of minority rights, diversion of funds and energy from other important goals and purposes of the system, and depletion of, or damage to, valuable natural resources."

The vertical lines in *Figure 5:2* do not indicate clear lines of demarcation. If one looks at any one of these columns it will be influenced to a greater or lesser extent (marked by a 2 or a 1 respectively) by the view that is represented in each of the headings.

		Philoso-phical / Sociolo-gical 1	Mumford 2	Sociolo-gical/ econo-mic 3	Causal logical Mathe-matical 4	Problem Expert oriented 5	General Living Systems Theory 6
Matter	Structure	1	1	2	2	1	2
	Process	1	1	1	1	1	2
Energy	Structure	1	1	2	2	1	2
	Process	1	1	1	2	1	2
Information	Structure	1	1	1	1	1	2
	Process	1	1	1	1	1	2
Model	Descriptive	2	2	2	2	1	2
	Prescriptive	2	2	1	1	1	1
Planning	Dynamic	1	2	1	1	1	2
System	Living	1	2	1	1	1	2
	Homeostatic	1	2	1	1	1	2
	Purposeful	2	2	1	1	1	2
	Causal-Logic	1	1	2	2	1	1
Theory	Hypothesis	1	1	1	2	1	2
	Emp.verification	1	1	2	2	2	2
	Validation	1	1	2	2	1	2
Philosophical		2	2	1	1	1	1
Cybernetics	Inform. flow	1	1	1	1	1	2
	Inform. capacity	1	1	1	1	1	2
Decider subsystem		1	2	1	1	1	2
	Aesthetics	2	2	1	1	1	1
	Ethics	2	2	1	1	1	1
	Quality of life	2	2	1	1	1	2

Figure 5:2 Comparison between different theories and GLST. T. Frandberg 1986.

The first column refers to Ulrich (1983).

The second column is represented by Mumford (1938).

The third column analyses sociological/ economic theories by Hermerén et al (1981) and Andersson, Samartin and Martinez (1983).

The fourth column is based on a trend where the causal connection in reality may be described by means of mathematical equations Lundqvist (1983).

The fifth column covers by a number of partial descriptions made by experts who represent different subjects and fields of experience, with reference to an agreed plan and goal. Swedish Council for Building Research (D6:1979).

Finally, the sixth column represents GLST.

To return once again to Heinz Pagels, one should try to create a "phenomenological model" that can be quantified. Living Systems is such a "model" that can provide the basis for a quantifiable model. Use of a simulation program allows representatives of different interests to sit in front of a model and see what their proposals for changes lead to in quantifiable terms. Different interests may for example be related to differing normative conceptions of economic life. These differences may depend for instance on seeing economic systems as either inherently unstable, tending to equilibrium, or, as in the case of Keynesianism, requiring instititutional reforms of a kind which facilitate rather than obstruct the capacity of the economy to function "normally".

Such assumptions are linked to a normative commitment to rational choice or decision making in economic affairs by means of devices like cost-benefit analysis. The aim of economic theory is therefore to find rational solutions for economic problems on the normative assumption that what the rational man would do the plain man should do.

What Morgan (1986) says (p. 134) is worth noting in comparison with what is said about rationality in Ulrich (1983):

> "Modern organizations are sustained by belief systems that emphasize the importance of rationality. Their legitimacy in the public eye often depends on their ability to demonstrate rationality. It is for this reason that anthropologists often refer to rationality as the myth of modern society. For like a primitive myth, it provides us with a comprehensive frame of reference, or structure of belief through which we can make day to day experience intelligible. The myth of rationality helps us to see certain

> patterns of action as legitimate, credible, and normal, hence to avoid the wrangling and debate that would arise if we were to recognize the basic uncertainty and ambiguity underlying many of our values and actions. One of the major strengths of the culture metaphor rests in the fact that it directs attention to the symbolic or even "magical" significance of even the most rational aspects of organization life."

In the above passage Morgan does not display the same conviction as Ulrich does regarding the content of the concept of rationality; he sees the task of the theory being to illuminate how certain internal adjustments to key variables may enhance "rational" planning. This approach has a technocratic rather than social theoretical bias: where it does not explain, it shows men how to do better. The fact that thinkers then resort to more or less theoretical reasoning (which cannot be directly linked to how one is to proceed) merely serves to blur the picture of the working method and thinking one has found usable. The question of the differences between the research undertaken within natural science and that undertaken within social science has been discussed in for example Pagels (1988) and Capra (1982).

CONCLUSION

Large administrative systems tend to become more and more complex, not directly because of the involvement of persons who frame rules and regulations but because of an obviously inherent characteristic of such systems, especially where social planning is concerned. In many cases such administrative systems no longer function in the way originally intended but have constantly to be reorganized and enlarged in order to minimize the unintended consequences that side effects can have. Stafford Beer has in Behavioral Science (1973) illustrated the problem in the article "The World We Manage".

Chapter 6

COMPARISONS BETWEEN DIFFERENT SYSTEM MODELS

INTRODUCTION

In this chapter different approaches of describing models of reality are compared. There follow examples of models which shed light on advantages and drawbacks where simulation has been undertaken. The chapter gives an account of the current examples over and above those shown at each level in Miller (1978 p. 85), where he supplies four possible classes of models and simulations:

(a) nonliving artifacts
(b) living, usually human, representations
(c) models in words, numbers, or other symbols, including computer programs
(d) living system - computer interactions.

The one which is used here belongs mainly to class (d) living system-computer interactions. Examples of comparisons have been drawn from the following list: Forrester (1969), Cellier (1982), Chadwick (1978), Cellier (1982) Leimkühler, Warfield (1976), Klir (1985), De Greene (1973), de Rosnay (1975), Pattee in Langton (1989), House and McLeod (1977), Zeigler and Weinberg (1970), Mikulecky (1983), Mader (1988), Liljenström (1987).

SIMULATION, MODEL, AND UNCERTAINTY

There is in Forrester (1969) no information-processing subsystem and as a result the residents are in this case given little opportunity of taking part in the decision-making process. Forrester says that his book is more of an opening of a subject than it is a package of final results and recommendations. This is in line with the commentary from Cellier (1982) where it is maintained that examples of how to set about simulation are given all too often, but that information about the results obtained and how these are to be verified and validated by others appears all too rarely. This presentation is also limited in this way but has a wider application in that it deals with the question of how structuring and quantification are to be carried out according to GLST and also treats the questions of validation and verification.

In the section "Systems Dynamics" (p. 120) Cellier (1982) by J. D. Lebel it is claimed that "Systems Dynamics" is a way of describing those complex systems that constitute a line of demarcation between science and society. Lebel maintains that "Systems Dynamics" aims to narrow the gap by providing opportunities for analysis, synthesis and a language for processing complex systems. Lebel's conclusion is that systems dynamics must be applied by the person who wishes to understand its possibilities. This, in principle, is the same argument for simulation as I advance here. The list of references in Cellier 1982 covers more than 700 items of which 60 are books. Rosnay (1975 p. 82) writes — that simulation is only one approach among many, a complementary method of studying complex systems and he goes on to see (p. 82) the danger of too much freedom in the choice of variables and a risk of becoming lost in the infinity of variables.

> "The results of simulation must not be confused with reality (as is often the case) but, compared with what one knows of reality, should be used as the basis for the possible modification of the initial model. When one continues to use such a process in successive approximations, the usefulness of simulation will become apparent."

He says that models are imperfect but however, the only alternatives are "mental models" made from fragments of elements and intuitive thinking. De Rosnay stresses the danger of too much freedom that may be due to the choice of the model, something that I also have noted.

In Langton (1989 p. 66) – "Simulations, Realizations, and Theories of Life", Howard H. Pattee puts forward the views expressed in the following sentences which are in agreement with the view of simulation that lies behind the present simulation. "For these reasons (which he previously described), there is never any doubt that the simulation, no matter how accurate, is not the same as the thing simulated. Of course, the choice of what aspects of a system are simulated depends on what is considered significant, and significance cannot be isolated from one's knowledge and theory of the system. Lacking a conceptual theory, a good simulation at least must represent the essential functions of a realization of the system.

I consider it important to provide an opportunity of shedding light on what the uncertainties consist of and so improve the likelihood that the result can be communicated.

SIMULATION AND QUALITIES OF EARLIER AND FUTURE MODELS

My aim is also to remedy the deficiencies highlighted by what Chadwick (1978 p. 403) writes in the following sentence (concerning System Dynamics a la Forrester) – where he says that system dynamics has been oversold, and that it is now being undersold; he expects that systems dynamics should soon be emerging, when further reinforcement by attempts at operational use are made. He adds on (p. xv) some limitations where he sees the planning process as bounded by rationality, which involves human judgements as well as rational arguments, and points out that it is irrational to expect the planning process to be wholly rational. Warfield (1976 p. 50) is aware of the problems, concerning bounded rationality, when he writes that it is important to note the demands emanating from the current thinking within different fields such as philosophy, social science and technology.

Whitehead's thoughts about systems stem from a point earlier in time as well as being on a more comprehensive level. Whitehead, quoted in Warfield (1976 p. 165), described speculative philosophy in a way which nowadays can be seen as the endeavour to frame a coherent, logical, necessary system of general ideas of which our experience can be interpreted as one of the characteristics of systems science "not one of the sciences, but rather a survey of the sciences which aims at interconnecting, harmonizing, and completing them. It confronts the sciences with each other and with concrete facts." Cosmology deals with the universe as an orderly system. The ideal would thus be a single cosmology unifying the many sciences. However, Whitehead maintained that philosophy is not built up from a foundation of clear and distinct ideas, and that we are not arguing from well defined premises. interdisciplinary approach which characterizes GLST. (p. 41)

Leimkühler in Cellier (1982 p. 63) supplies some methodological problems in energy modelling, in an historical survey of the use of simulation models. In so doing he summarizes the objections raised against the first generation models, "Simple System-Dynamics' (SD) Models, including Forrester's World Models and Meadows' "The Limits to Growth". The model behavior was rather erratic. This was basically due to the fact that too many variables were connected, their structure were impenetrable, and the external assumptions were based on too few and ill-documented data of the kind used for tuning the models. He further pointed out that the programming language had deficiencies and the econometric and statistical methods were lacking models. Leimkühler then describes the second generation models that he mentions – Mesarovic/Pestel (MP) Models – and much of the criticism directed against the first generation also applies to the second generation models. He goes on to mention the following general postulates for simulation modelling: there is no substitute for model transparency. The model structure should be explainable to and understandable by any external user who is accustomed to the real system the model is designed to reflect. Leimkühler then adds (p. 71)

> "On the applications side, one will hopefully be able to notice the disappearance of today's disjunction between designers on one side and decision-makers on the other, being replaced by an intensive long-term, close discussion guided by goodwill from both sides. This would make the frequent complaints about irrelevance of modelling efforts and/or non-participation in the design process"

As was noted earlier the purpose here is in line with the aim of removing the reasons for the above complaints. The aim is as far as possible to avoid the weaknesses Leimkühler points to, and to encourage people to display increasing interest in taking part in the decision-making process. Klir (1985) is of the same opinion that the philosophy of the expert system he referred to as the General Systems Problem Solver, or GSPS, is to allow the user to define his own order of preference for the systems under consideration. This paragraph is in agreement with what GLST is aiming at — the important difference being that ordering takes place while taking into account the conditions which apply in respect of living systems and meets the requirements laid down below by Klir (1985 p. 180): "It is interesting to consider whether one can have a measure for the degree of wholeness of a system. One can, of course, always draw a distinction, make a mark, and get a "system", but the result does not always seem to be equally a "whole system", a "natural entity" or" a coherent object" or "concept". The above viewpoints concerning wholeness and other aspects are taken into account in GLST, where the degree of wholeness is viewed in the context of simulation of the conditions for the survival of the system.

SIMULATION AS AN AID IN COMMUNICATION

Nearly 20 years ago De Greene 1973 emphasized (as did Sir Geoffrey Vickers (1970), Beer (1979), and others what today is clearly all the more necessary, namely, (p. 325) before time runs out, to assess the state of the world and begin better managing the world. De Greene (1973 p. 401) says that the questions he has taken up are not the only ones (though he puts forward) and urges the reader as far as he is able to work for a better understanding of decision-making situations

1. Who takes the decisions?
2. Questions concerning values, valuations and motivation - how are these to be changed for the better?
3. How are we to prevent the negative effect of conflicts of interest, the fragmentation of our view of the world?
4. How are we to ensure the implementation of the changes that result from changes in valuations, in behavior and from new teaching methods?
5. How are we to ensure that the results of scientific studies and analyses encourage people to bring about improvements?

Of the above questions, those which touch on how we are to be able to prevent the fragmentation of our view of the world, and how scientific results can be used to encourage people to bring about improvements, are the ones which lie closest to the objective of this present simulation of Living Systems. De Greene presents a thorough and comprehensive account of possibilities and limitations where "factors in analysis, design and management" are concerned. He lists (p. 68) 20 different points involving negative criticism of the approach employed by Forrester and those in the same category. In point 21 he writes -"the main contribution may be on its greater emphasis on the system as a whole. The main value may be in terms of generalizations which stimulate others to validate and to find specifics." This final point is sufficient to justify continued work on the proposed application of Living Systems. It also stresses the importance of stimulating people to participate in the social debate. It has become evident that a large percentage of the population of the world now rank environmental issues as a high priority. This may be seen partly as a result of current research into environmental issues and as an example of how the questions 1- 5 listed above can be answered.

In "Factors in looking at Sociotechnical Systems" (p. 266) 16 points are noted in order to point to "the most meaningful approach to the study of complex sociotechnical systems, namely, the recognition of interrelationships among cities, transportation, health, education, power generation, etc. in the ecological, social, and political (power) environments." GLST has in these respects a conceptual system which makes it possible to describe connections between the cell and the Earth on the basis of a theory about survival. Several of the questions deal with "degrees of openness and changes", thermodynamics, equifinality, a comparison of "simulation models" with "analytical models", and the gathering and processing of data dealt with in my presentation. One has to be aware that a mathematical description of the relationships in the model can yield results that go through the same point with different assumptions concerning the initial position, owing to the complex situation that is being examined. Possibly the most valuable thing would be if the use of models could lead to a discussion of the advantages and drawbacks and in this way help to promote the continued development and understanding of urban models and living systems.

EXAMPLES OF CELL MODELS

The four references Zeigler (1970), Mikulecky (1983), Mader (1988), and Liljenström (1987) have common features in that they describe the cell with the help of models of structure and function. They also exhibit great similarities with the approach and procedures employed in the simulation of Living Systems carried out here. They apply a systems view in the building up of the models. The connections between subsystems of the model are described mainly with first order differential equations of the cell as a living system. In their structure the models and approaches are basically similar to GLST and to the simulation applied here. Mikulecky observes that the method he uses in order to describe network modelling and simulation corresponds to that of the living system. He goes on to point out that it is now possible to simulate complicated multicellular epithelial membranes with channels and/or carriers in certain selected membranes. He also draws attention to the need to acquire experimentally verified data to insert into the model. The need to describe the cell membrane and its various functions is particularly relevant when the task to be undertaking is the cross-level analysis of extruder. Co-ordination between the building of theoretical models and the carrying out of experiments designed to generate bases for models could be well worthwhile. Liljenström (1987) takes up the difference between closed and open systems where open systems function a long way from equilibrium as a result of the dissipation of free energy from their environment. A living system can in this way reduce its own entropy at the expense of an increase of the entropy in its environment. The significance of the above is that the entropy created by the systems at each level stays within the boundary of the Earth (biosphere and atmosphere) when the Earth is viewed as a practically closed system. Like Mikulecky, Liljenström emphasises the importance of ensuring that there is an exchange (of ideas) as a result of the experience that can be acquired by building theoretical models and carrying out experiments. Liljenström (1987) notes (p. 25) that "the best description of a real system or process, is obtained with analytic expressions and equations," In many cases, though, the system and its processes are so complex that it is impossible to handle them analytically, and then computer simulation is the only possible method. As Mikulecky points out, it is important that the simulation program is user-friendly. The program employed, where the mathematical connections between subsystems are described in a digraph as in ITHINK and STELLA, ensures clearness and is easy to handle using the control functions built into the programme.

Bernhard P. Zeigler and Roger Weinberg make use of a model that describes a metabolic network in order to study the global operation of the cell. This, they maintain, is an important difference compared with other models which do not aim to make a comparison between the behavior of the model and real cell behavior and which study limited parts of the behavior of the cell. In accordance with *Figure 9:2*, which shows subsystems and their connections at different levels, and also with the supply in *Figure 12:11,* the intention is to study the subsystems and their connections within the whole. As in Zeigler and Weinberg the connections between the parts are expressed in difference equations. Zeigler and Weinberg also point out that systems theory concepts facilitate the understanding and formulation of problems for biologists as well as other scientists; this is in accordance with GLST, where the approach adopted and the application of methods that can be used across the boundaries of different fields of science are of fundamental importance.

A similar approach is mentioned in an interview with Christopher Langton in Omnis, Langton (1991), where he says that those working at the Complex Systems Group Theoretical Division, Los Alamos are going to try: "to capture the cell's behaviour while it incorporates stuff from the outside, taking in metabolites and turning them into cell constituents, turns genetic code into entities that move around inside the cell and make it do things like divide, produce offspring with variants, and die."

Having discussed models and their design I will now proceed to illustrate properties which are generally important in building of models.

Chapter 7

MODEL BUILDING

INTRODUCTION

As an introduction to the description of the properties of the models, the following quotation is taken from Funtowitz and Ravetz (p. 151): Funtowitcz and Ravetz point to the need for meeting the challenges of global environmental issues by saying (p. 151)

> "We have now reached a point where a narrow scientific tradition is no longer appropriate to our needs. Unless we find a way of enriching our science to include practice, we will fail to create methods for coping with the environmental challenges, in all their complexity, variability and uncertainty." This approach present the possibility of confirming many of the hypotheses put forward by Miller has stated and is also in line with what Miller argues when he says that some can probably be confirmed but (p. 114) "undoubtedly others are entirely wrong or subject to various qualifications and restrictions, since more contradicting than sustaining instances can be found"

DIFFERENT POINTS OF VIEW

Kenneth Boulding

Boulding sees two sides of General Systems — General General Systems which lie nearer to philosophy and Special General Systems which are near to mathematics and computer aided model building and are in line with the approach adopted here. He points to the importance of understanding that not everything can be regarded as systematic and of not seeing order that does not exist. He also sees a danger in building systems with constant parameters since there is then a danger that we will not become aware that changes take place. He sees "sensitivity analysis" as valuable because it provides an opportunity of studying the effects of small changes in parameters, which is also one of my intentions.

Miller

Miller distinguishes between three kinds of models (p. 85):

1. isomorphism, a formal identity between two conceptual systems,
2. homology, a formal identity between two concrete systems,
3. a formal identity between a conceptual system and a concrete (or an abstracted) system.

He regards simulation as a separate class of model that shows changes in processes similar to those that occur in "the referent system". The term simulation is used here in the sense in which it is used by GLST. The model sees an entity into which knowledge that is acquired through separate models can be inserted. This is an attempt to prevent the emergence of the problems which, as Aulin (1989) shows, can arise when models are constructed without a solid scientific foundation. It is also an attempt to achieve a dynamic model such as Nicolis and Prigogine (1989) refer to when they say that the adaptive possibility of societies is the main factor which enables them to survive in the long run, and that dynamic modelling is one way of describing this interaction.

Milan Zeleny

Milan Zeleny expresses a dissenting opinion in the following passage from ISSS meeting (1989 p. 149) "Unfortunately, the "proper" methodology of social sciences still remains retarded and relatively undeveloped, dominated by differential equations, calculus, statistics, econometrics and other tools of physics. These tools may be applicable to all kinds of socially engineered "perestroikas" and man-made social systems in general, but they fail to adequately model the spontaneous social order and the natural, self-organizing world as such." He then adds: "The traditional norms of reason, guiding the imposition and subsequent restructuring of socialism, embody a naive and uncritical theory of rationality, an obsolete and unscientific methodology."

Sven Erik Jorgensen

Sven Erik Jorgensen distinguishes in Mitsch (1989 p. 49) between 17 classes of models in "Principles of Ecological Modelling", where the model I have used here can be assigned to "Research Models" and "Dynamic Models".

Kenneth Bailey

Kenneth Bailey writes that by building a sufficiently extensive model we can safeguard the potential for studying both rational and random action, both process and product, both positivism and idealism. GLST is an alternative way of attempting to fulfil the requirements for a good explanation approach to model construction set forth by Bailey and White (1989). Bailey (1990) says that the attempt to build successful models of complex social systems encounters many obstacles, one of which involves meeting objections that systems analyses make use of analogies with organisms or mechanical systems, and that they are deterministic. He goes on to say (p. 106) that macrosociological systems models often fall prey to the criticism that they exhibit "determinism" of some sort or another (biological, economic, environmental etc.).

In a global state of affairs which now demands an understanding of a hyper-complex situation, the above characteristics of this systems approach would be extremely valuable if they could be applied. Of course, it is possible to raise objections for example to the extent to which, sociological terms are tenable. Nagel (1961 p. 447-502) does not regard this route as all that fruitful. This is illustrated, for example, by the point made in Checkland (1988 p. 77) where he criticizes "also the use of the living organism as an analogy or metaphor for other larger entities such as families, societies, and civilizations. This is a metaphor which — as I shall argue later — has been very bad for social science." By using structures and processes of matter-energy and information according to GLST one can handle the objections which are pointed to in Bailey's final point above and also Checkland's objections. Today, it is increasingly important to describe the connection between the conditions for society and those for the survival of cells and organisms and how, for example, road traffic is a function of the interaction between housing, population, industry and commerce and communication at different levels.

Conclusion

If one interprets the behaviour of a living system as rational then this means that thc behavior is interpreted rationally in the context in which the system exists; in this case as a living system. But nowadays it does not seem possible to describe living systems at a generally higher level as deterministic and rational. An extensive list of literature is included in "Dynamics and Control of Structures" by Meirowitch (1990).

Connections between Model and Reality

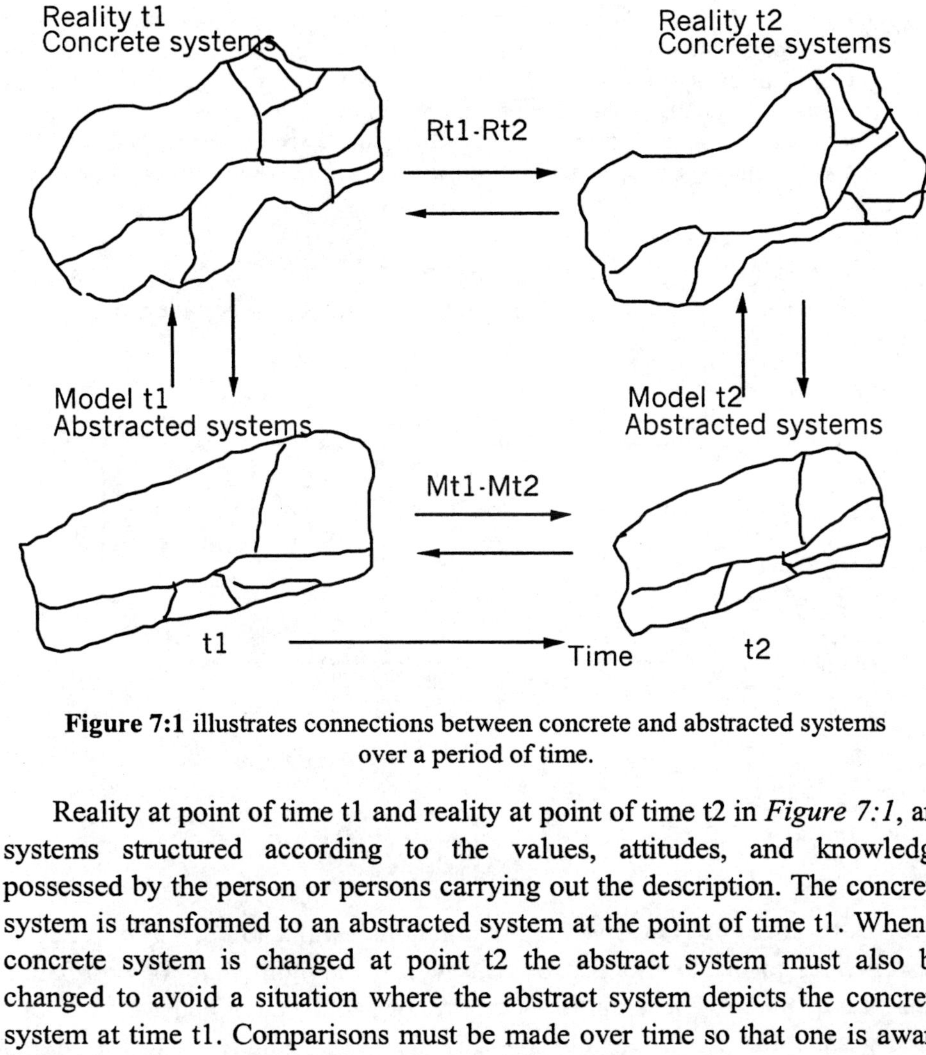

Figure 7:1 illustrates connections between concrete and abstracted systems over a period of time.

Reality at point of time t1 and reality at point of time t2 in *Figure 7:1*, are systems structured according to the values, attitudes, and knowledge possessed by the person or persons carrying out the description. The concrete system is transformed to an abstracted system at the point of time t1. When a concrete system is changed at point t2 the abstract system must also be changed to avoid a situation where the abstract system depicts the concrete system at time t1. Comparisons must be made over time so that one is aware of changes in concrete and abstracted systems. In Bailey (1990 p. 21) Miller is quoted thus:

> "Science advances as the formal identity or isomorphism increases between a theoretical conceptual system and objective findings about concrete or abstracted systems" The model is built up from one or more fields of knowledge as understood by the designer. The symbols used denote critical

subsystems in "the abstracted system" are built up according to the conceptual system contributed by Living Systems. The relationships are described with the aid of difference equations and qualitative simulation according to *Figure 12:16* with the symbols and arrows constituted by GLST. Simulation of any system implies a mapping from the observable aspects of the system to corresponding symbolic elements of the simulation. This mapping is called measurement in physics and in most other sciences. Since measurement can never be made with absolute accuracy, the quality of simulations must be judged by additional criteria based on a theory of the system.

In Bobrow (1985) Benjamin Kuipers (p. 171) shows *Figure 7:2* which can be used together with *Figure 7:1* to show the connection between model and reality.

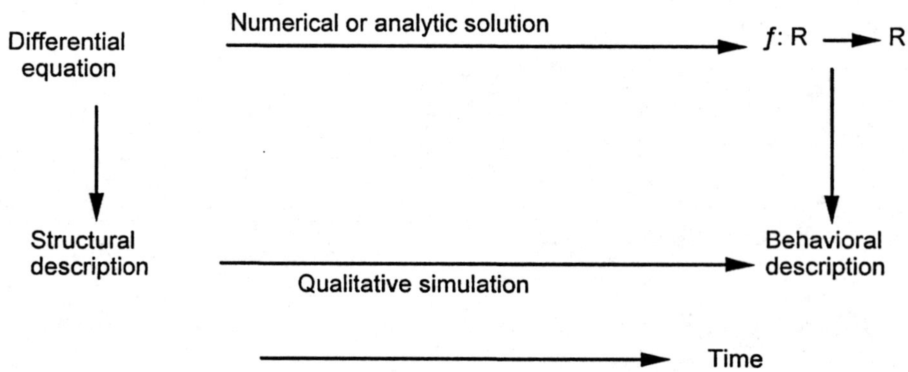

Figure 7:2 Behavioral description studied by means of analytic solution and qualitative simulation. Source Bobrow (1985). A time axis has been added here.

The meaning of "Qualitative simulation" is similar to what Heinz Pagels describes as phenomenological models which are significant for correlating data in a quantitative, descriptive way, without going into deeper reason why such correlations exist. In Hall and Day (1977 p. 9) there is also a similar differentiation between analytical modelling which makes use of relatively complicated mathematics, and simulation modelling characterized by use of relatively simple mathematics together with computers.

An unambiguous description of the implications of the concept of objectivity, which basically is a philosophical question, is likely to be very difficult when it is not restricted to a part of reality (mainly within the natural sciences) where experiments are likely to be most easily performed, validated and verified. Objectivity is here regarded as meaning that those who carry out the same experiment must come up with the same result. For instance, experts in the debate about the traffic situation are in many situations far from being agreed on how the situation is to be described and interpreted. This is another way of expressing the characteristics of a pluralist society. The creator of the image has captured some aspect of the object's essence. He can tell us verbally how he reduced nature to formulas, numbers, methods. But by expressing nature in such terms, it becomes dry, stripped of meaning and spirit. The language of imagery is more universal than the language of words and symbols. There is a dilemma because objectivity expresses less than subjectivity.

Nagel (1986) has given an exhaustive alternative for the attempt to elucidate the difference between subjectivity and objectivity. He concludes his book (p. 231): "The objective standpoint can't really be domesticated. Not only does it threaten to leave us behind, but it gives us more than we can take on in real life. When we acknowledge our containment in the world, it becomes clear that we are incapable of living in the full light of that acknowledgement. Our problem has in this sense no solution, but to recognize that is to come as near we can to living in light of the truth." According to what is maintained below there is no guarantee that the image creator under changing conditions over time knows how he/she reduced nature to formulas etc. The situation is similar to that which prevails when it comes to deciding how the connection between values and decisions is to be described. It can also be seen as a parallel to the question of the connection between mind and matter. At one extreme, we have those who say that measurement is completed at the sensory transducers, and that all the rest is symbol manipulation. At the other extreme are physicists who consider the consciousness of the observer as the ultimate termination of a measurement. A more common view is that neural cell assemblies that are large enough to be feature detectors may be said to measure events, but we are still a long way from consensus on a theory of perception or a theory of measurement which influences the acquiring, processing, storage and retrieval of data. In Langton (1989) (p. 262), Oppenheimer says:

> "Hierarchical structures abound in human societies. They range from consciously man-made corporate hierarchies to spontaneously emerging

community, neighbourhood, family, individual relationships. From urban plans, to mental thought processes, and beyond - down to the innermost fabric of our flesh. Spanning a continuum, these societal groupings provide a bridge between natural and artificial. Recursively organized, they provide efficient conduits to resources, information and other human needs."

MODEL AND EMERGENTS

The description of connections between model and reality is complicated by the conditions that touch on emergents where Miller (1978 p. 28) sees emergents as a quality resulting from the fact that more complex systems at higher levels manifest characteristics which differ from the sum of the characteristics of the units observed at lower levels. He opposes any conceptualization of emergents that involves inscrutable characteristics of the whole, greater than the sum of its parts, which are not susceptible to the ordinary method of scientific analysis. The view is in line with that presented by H. H. Pattee in Langton (1989 p. 71) as follows: "However, with the popularization of mathematical models of complex morphogeneses, such as Thom's catastrophe theory, Prigogine's dissipative structures and Mandelbrot's fractals, and the more profound recognition of the generality of symmetry-breaking instabilities and chaotic dynamics, the concept of emergence has become scientifically respectable."

The following expresses another view which differs somewhat (from what he has said in the first sentences in this section) where he sees consciousness and emergence as lying outside the domain of scientific theory. Both consciousness and emergence can be treated as inherently weak concepts, that is as currently perceived illusions resulting from our ignorance of how things really work, i.e. lack of data or incomplete theories. The history of science in one sense supports this view as more and more of these mysteries yield to empirical exploration and theoretical description. One, therefore, could claim that consciousness and emergence are just our names for those areas of awareness that are at present lying outside the domain of scientific theory. Miller (1978 p. 716) says in the context of "Organization" that variables of human satisfaction, feelings, motivations, effectiveness, and interpersonal reactions have little place in current mathematical models and computerized simulations of organizations. The chief reason for this is perhaps being that these variables are difficult to quantify. As a biologist, De Duve (1984 p. 17) says something that is asserted especially in social science and within a field such as physics.

> "There is no such thing as an isolated fact. There are only recordings and interpretations of facts by individuals. Even the simplest observations come to us through our senses, which act as highly selective, as well as subjective, filters that let through only certain limited aspects of reality. We have greatly extended the range of our senses by means of instruments, but only at the cost of interposing additional filters."

This helps us to see why it is very difficult to conceptualize emergents which are not susceptible to ordinary methods of scientific analysis. Miller admits (p. 1025) that: "The fit between the conceptual system and the empirical findings reported in this book appears poorest at the highest two or three levels."

CAUSE, EFFECT AND EMERGENCE

Ayres (1978) takes up the question of causal connections in quantifiable relationships within economics. He points to the risks that arise when multiple correlation (and regression) methods are used uncritically, for example, when multiple correlation analysis (based on fuel consumption during a number of years) is used as the only method of forecasting energy consumption. He shows that there is a need for non-statistical information, whether theoretical or empirical or whether derived from other disciplines or from other branches of economics. He supplies examples of how this interdisciplinary fusion can be accomplished in the construction of "large-scale realistic" economic models for policy analysis. The discussion of connections between cause and effect can be widened to include the discussion of the connection between mind and matter as in Popper, Eccles (1977), where the problem of parallelism is taken up. Cohen (1931) brings up "The principle of sufficient reason" and observes (p. 150): "Everything is connected in definite ways with definite other things, so that its full nature is not revealed except by its position and relations within a system."

Broad (1925), unlike Miller and Vandervert, sees understanding of how emergent properties are dependent on relations between cause and effect as being more remote in time. The problem involved in finding relations between cause and effect can be linked to the problem of understanding emergent properties. The difficulties of understanding how and when emergent properties arise can be illustrated in Briggs and Peat (1990 p. 144). *Figure 7:3* shows bifurcation (branching) points in the system's changes in terms of the horizontal axis of disequilibrium flux and the vertical axis of solutions. The figure aims to illustrate that though the causality operates at every instant, branching takes place unpredictably. An example of a bifurcation point is given by Prigogine when the earth "escaped" to a higher form of order by evolving an oxygen-using form of life. This example corresponds to the view that the earth can be seen as a living system.

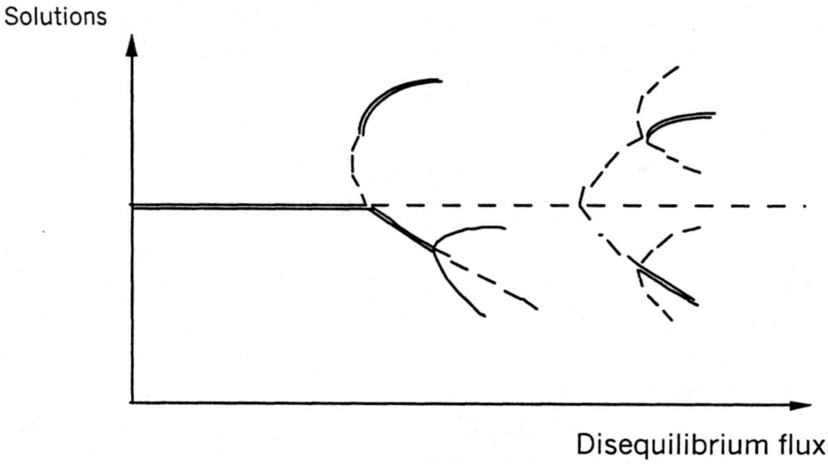

Figure 7:3 Solutions along the axis of disequilibrium flux Briggs and Peat 1990

He is not of the opinion that the increasing environmental costs of the entropic build-up have been taken into account in models that describe how one can optimally extract, for example, metals or fuels from natural resources – or in one word, extract negentropy, – which is also pointed out in Chapter 8 on economics. Problems arise when one has to explain the connection between cause and effect on the one hand and the situation that has arisen on the other. The whole is more than the sum of the parts. There are many examples of how people have failed to see the connection between the constituent parts and the final result of, say, planning.

It appears that it will to some extent usually be possible to trace the result caused by the parts, and on such occasions one says, for example, that a certain part is due to how co-ordination took place in the structures and processes one has observed. The rest of the result is due to factors that lie in the surroundings, or else to factors that are found within the structure but cannot be attributed to quantifiable entities.

Finding a formalized connection between cause and effect is a difficult problem (if it can in fact be done at all). The number of possible variables is often large, and then one is faced with the task of selecting a certain number of them. Which variables in a given situation yield the best interpretation (explanation) of cause and effect? The real problem is finding the variables that provide the best possibility of making predictions about the future. In this situation one tends to prefer, or is more or less obliged to choose, the variables that are the most accessible and the easiest to measure. Apart from the problems involved in understanding the formalized connection ("The language of mathematics is a theoretical language, but it is not the same as causal language") between the variables, the situation gives rise to another problem: How is one to describe the connection between the variables selected for inclusion in the formalized description and those that lie outside? The situation has been described in Blalock (1964 p. 173) where, he writes:

> "Causality is conceived in the present work as involving the notion of prediction, i.e. producing effects. This kind of notion is difficult to formalize, as in mathematical or logical systems. Nor is it subject to empirical verification. The notion of production introduces asymmetry into causal relationships. Temporal sequences are also symmetrical but should not be confused with causal relationships. Nor should causality be confused with prediction, which refers to the state of the observer's knowledge."

and (p. 85) a direct relationship can be transformed into an indirect one by inserting an intervening variable. Lovelock (1988) has named Gaia as a living system which describes a living, evolving, self-regulating, self-organizing life form. Although his thoughts have been called into question they have provoked an intriguing debate concerning the conditions for the survival of the earth.

He goes on to refer to what Prigogine calls a new uncertainty principle which says that beyond a certain threshold of complexity, systems go in unpredictable directions; they lose their initial conditions and cannot be reversed or recovered. And they conclude that a modeller is not able to control the complex system by quantifying it and mastering its complexity; she/he needs to increase her "intuitions" about how the system works so she/he can interact with it more harmoniously. The relation between cause and effect can then be described as knowledge embracing theories and methods which enables one to make predictions as in Blalock (1964) according to the above. Bronowski (1965) also sees the problem inherent in the situation that a proposition about arithmetic is expressed as a proposition in arithmetic.

For this reason there is no sharp line between the result obtained when a cause-effect connection is described by means of an algorithm or when it is not. Algorithms in both experimental and non experimental situations are limited by their lack of completeness and consistency. In the end the interpretation of the connection between cause and effect also becomes a question of experience and knowledge. The simulation facilitates processing, but without for that reason becoming getting stuck in the connections between variables that are assumed in mathematical equations such as regression analysis.

Acquiring and Processing Data

How is one to acquire, process, store and retrieve data in order to be able, through simulation, to handle such a complicated structure and such complex processes as those taking place for example in a cell? The question is even more justified when it is a matter of the community and the Earth, which have greater complexity, for one thing because of the existence of the decision processes which take place there. Also, how is one to find data that describe the interplay, or perhaps more correctly, the effects that are to be found within and between these levels?

De Greene (1973) (p. 206) gives a list of the problems in the area of system and simulation, and their relationships to data.

1. Knowledge of the state of the system may be inadequate,
2. System identification techniques may be limited,
3. Data to substantiate a large model may be absent or difficult or impossible to acquire,
4. Available data may be "noisy",
5. Large systems may transcend our ability,
6. Criterion functions are hard to acquire,
7. Input-output models commonly used to express cause-effect relationships in engineering and economic systems may be grossly misleading,
8. Decomposition of complex systems into smaller more manageable systems may be by no means obvious,
9. Time scales may differ,
10. Physical scales may differ over hierarchical levels,
11. State variables may not have compatible dimensions.

This list has been reproduced because it is to a large part in agreement with my own experience of data processing in many connections, such as those concerned with energy evaluations of the effect and estimates of measures implemented by the state. The points listed are also closely related to what I have experienced from official statistics, which at the level of society have their origin in the ideas about national accounts which originally formed the basis for preparing a statistical report of a country's economic situation, and were the start of political economy. The collection of information was accordingly directed at those who proved to have assets that were needed in order to report on the income and expenditures of the state. According to Johannisson (1988) two opposing schools of thought appeared around the year 1800. On one hand were those who held the view that the description of a state could be reduced to figures giving the number of square kilometres, the capital assets, the number of inhabitants and domestic animals in columns. Against them were ranged those who were of the opinion that national spirit, a love of liberty, genius and character, which could not be reduced to figures, were the elements that best corresponded to a description of a country's strength. She describes the difference between the view of the world that reduced reality to quantifiable units within a deterministic view of the world, and those who, in the spirit of German Romanticism, held a basic view in which reality was regarded as complex and intangible. She adds that statistics and mathematical descriptions constitute the centre of gravity of the majority of present day studies. Karin Johannisson (1988 p. 186) says that the prognoses are taken as absolute truths and that they may be self-fulfilling. Mobility, complexity and challenges are held back right from the start. She ends her book by comparing the views of different welfare models currently prevailing in Sweden.

With reservations for the difficulty of making such a comparison she notes that past society, just like the present one, could be represented by rational goals in that a differentiation was made between the producers (the business community, the working population) and the consumers ("Public servants" and "The Idle Rich"). Neither is there such a great difference between the 18th century view where mercantilism was prepared to measure human dignity in terms of money and the view that human dignity today can be determined by means of a reasonable price. Johannisson points out that what is known as the Uppsala School (dating from the early 1900s) did not approve of any metaphysical arguments for rationality. The highest principle for right and morality was the overall social utility.

COSTS, EFFICIENCY AND EFFECTIVENESS

Where models are concerned, account must be taken of cost and time aspects, which can be of decisive importance. If data are acquired too late then expenditures and other sacrifices may be in vain. What matters is finding the section of the function where the collection and processing of data yield the best exchange. Langefors (1970) shows the relationship between the cost of simplifications, the degree of realism of the model used, and the total costs *Figure 7:4* (p. 228) and *Figure 11* (p. 240)

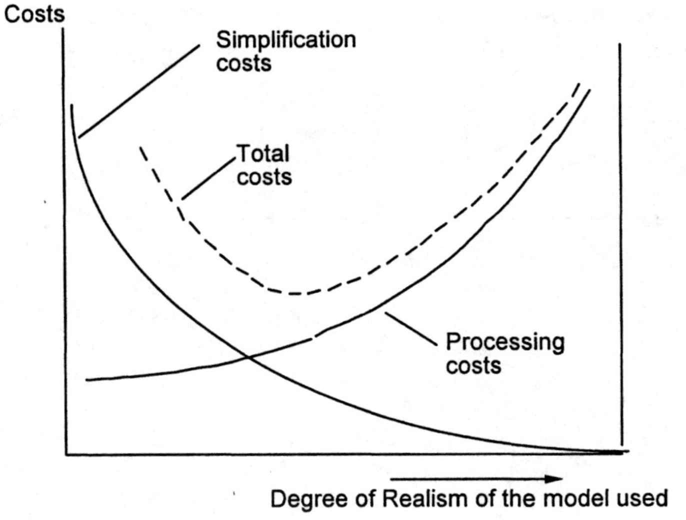

Figure 7:4 Relation between costs and degree of realism of the model used Source Langefors 1970

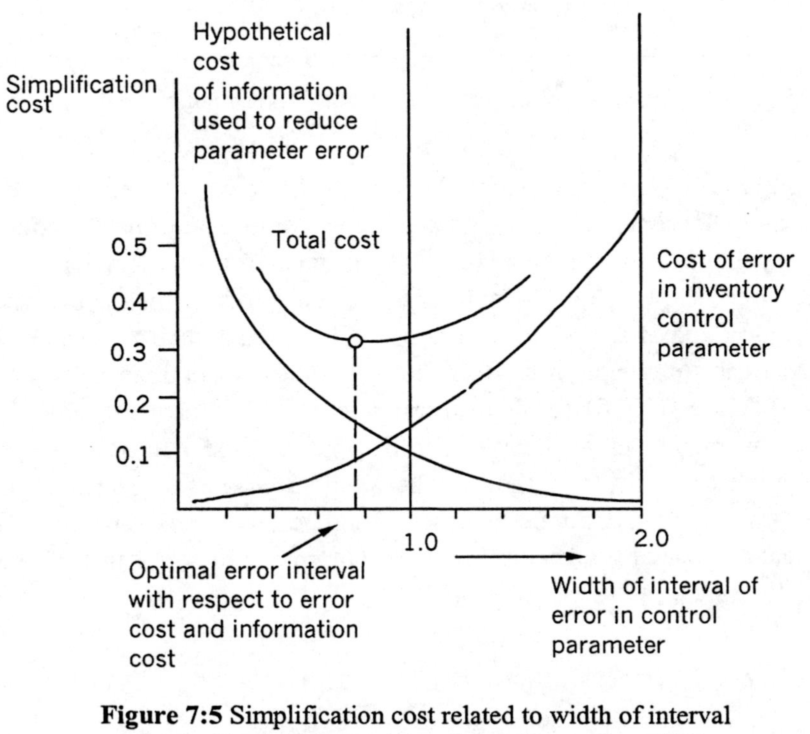

Figure 7:5 Simplification cost related to width of interval of error in control parameter. Source Langefors 1970.

Figure 7:6 from Mitsch and Jorgensen (1989 p. 54) supplements the cost picture depicted in *Figures 7:4* and *7:5*. Knowledge plotted versus model complexity measured, for example, by the number of state variables. Knowledge increases up to a certain level. Increased complexity beyond this level will not add to knowledge about the modelled system.

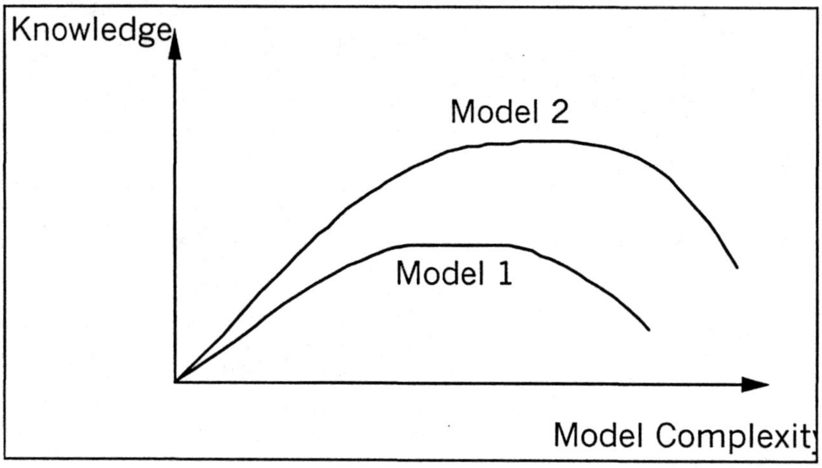

Figure 7:6 Knowledge related to model complexity. Source Mitsch and Jorgensen 1989.

In *Figure 7:6* the axis Model Complexity could also be exchanged for a Time axis. After a certain level has been reached the value of the model may decrease. The information comes too late to be useful in a decision situation, as the curves show. The cost must also be seen in relation to performance, latency, productivity, potentiability, capability and actuality, according to Stafford Beer's description in Beer (1979) of the connections between these concepts. Miller (1978) (p. 41) describes costs of adjustment processes as differing from one to another and from time to time. He sees a system's efficiency as determined by the ratio between success of its performance and the costs involved. Economic analyses of cost effectiveness are important in biological and social science but are more common and sophisticated in social than in biological sciences.

MEASUREMENT PROBLEMS AND LIMITS

Measurement problems are difficult to handle and solve, and not only within social science. In Lecomte de Noüy (1948) the point is made that measurement presents serious conceptual problems in physics, since it bridges the domains of known laws and unknown states of the system. Even in the classical theory of this bridge, and in quantum theory, the measurement problem is at present incomprehensible. In Wellburn (1988), under the heading "Thresholds and Injury", Allan Wellburn deals with the difficulty of determining which subjects have an effect that can be tolerated within the normal area for homeostasis (i.e. the internal self-regulation of cells or organisms) and those that have an injurious or lethal effect in the short or long run. He also looks at the problem of discovering changes which to begin with do not give any directly measurable effect, so that the adverse effects are seen only after some time. It can also be very difficult to demonstrate a clear connection between the agent of change and the change that results. In *Figure 7:7*, Wellburn (1988), a sigmoid curve is shown that describes the effect on plants that have been subjected to LD 50 (p. 14).

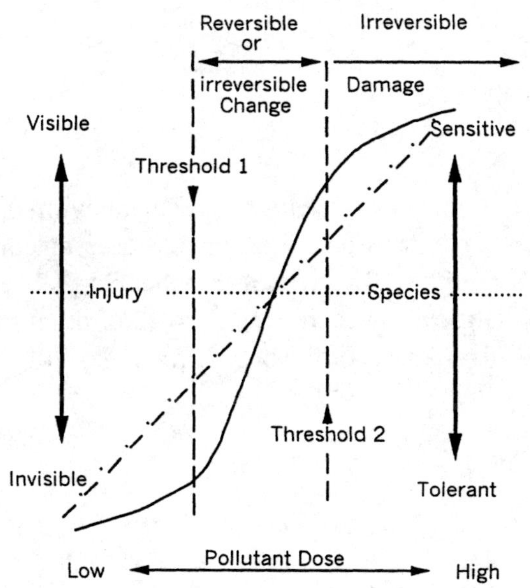

Figure 7:7 Effect on plants that have been subjected to LD 50. Source Wellburn 1988.

Figure 7:7 shows how difficult it is to determine the connections between an injurious influence and its effects. Where is the time limit between an irreversible and a reversible injury? Although providing an answer to this question might in most cases have to start from incomplete and uncertain measurement results the question still remains: How long is a decision concerning measures to be delayed?

A supplementary question then arises, namely: When is the connection so strongly documented, for example, through independently conducted experiments, that measures can be implemented? According to Wellburn the problems are connected with the following:

1. Knowledge of the state of the system may be inadequate.
2. System identification techniques may be limited.
3. Data to substantiate a large model may be absent or difficult or impossible to acquire.
4. Available data may be noisy.
5. Large systems transcend our ability.
6. Criterion functions are hard to acquire.
7. Input-output models, cause-effect relationships.
8. Decomposition
9. Time scales
10. Physical states may differ
11. State variables may not have compatible dimensions

The above points are in very close agreement with those listed by De Greene (p. 60), and have been included for purposes of comparison because they come from a scientist who represents biochemistry. The matrix in *Figure 7:8* taken from "Statistics Sweden" (1987 p. 26) describes how different substances affect different parts of the organism.

Known effects of some chemical substance and products

A Damage to nerves
B Tumours
C Damage to respiratory organs
D Damage to the liver and/or kidneys
E Blood diseases
F Heart and blood vessel diseases
G Skin damage
H Reduced fertility
I Miscarriage
J Genetic effects
K Damage to the foetus

	A	B	C	D	E	F	G	H	I	J	K
Heavy metals											
Cadmium		x	x	x	x	x		x	x		x
Lead	x			x	x			x	x		x
Mercury	x			x			x		x		x
Arsenic		x	x	x			x				x
Chromium		x	x				x				
Organic solvents											
Benzene	x	x			x						x
Toulene/xylene	x										x
Halogenized anaesthetic gases	x	x		x				x	x	x	x
Halogenized hydrocarbons											
Chloroprene	x		x	x	x			x	x	x	
Vinylchloride	x	x		x			x			x	
Trichlorethylene	x	x									
Ethylbromide		x	x	x				x			
PCB		x		x	x			x	x		
Tetrachlorethylene	x	x	x	x						x	x
Pesticides											
Carbaryl	x							x			
Kepon	x	x		x			x				
Carbon Disulphide	x					x		x	x		x
Carbon monoxide	x					x	x				x

Figure 7:8 Known effects of some chemical substances and products.
Source: Statistics Sweden 1987.

Figure 7:8 is an example of the above-mentioned complexity of a situation in which an attempt is made to see the connection between environmentally dangerous substances and damage to the cell, organ and organism. The situation becomes even more complex when one wishes to describe the connection between the levels from organization and upwards. This complexity is tackled in GLST through the use of the models and simulation proposed here, and is in line with an understanding of the situation that is presented in Nicolis and Prigogine (1989 p. 242): "The principal message of dynamic modelling advocated (in this section) is that the adaptive possibility of societies is the main source allowing them to survive in the long term, to innovate themselves, and to produce originality."

Figure 7:9 comes from Swedish Government Official Reports (1984:40 p. 23), and shows the connection between environment, pollution, traffic, diet, alcohol and drugs and tobacco, and various kinds of illnesses. It also shows the connections between structures and processes in living systems connections which GLST provides a basis for describing and quantifying by means of simulation according to STELLA. *Figure 7:9* contains descriptions of systems at different levels from the cell (tumours), organs (heart diseases), and organism (diseases of the manipulative organs) to organization (the physical working environment) and society (social environment during childhood).

	Heart-vascular diseases	Mental illness	Diseases of manipulative organs	Tumours	Injuries	Diseases of respiratory organs
Social environment during childhood	*	**				
Social working environment and unemployment	**	**			*	
Physical working environment		*	**	**	**	**
Social housing environment		*				
Physical housing environment				*	**	*
Air/water pollution				*	**	*
Traffic				*		*
Diet	**			**	**	*
Alcohol and drugs		**		*		*
Tobacco	**			**		*

Figure 7:9 Health policy matrix* denotes some connection ** denotes strong connection Source Swedish Government Official Reports 1984:40

Chapter 8

ENTROPY

INTRODUCTION

As one of the prerequisites here is that the Earth is regarded as a system which is moving towards increasing entropy, it is important to describe what is implied by the term entropy, taking into account the arguments for and against this point of view. The implication of entropy is also dependent on the way the difference between open and closed systems is defined.

The term has been assigned different meanings in different connections. In Miller (1978 p. 13) under basic concepts, entropy is an epitomization which shows 13 relationships between information and entropy, form and chaos, information and uncertainty, signal and noise, order and disorder. Although matter-energy and information always flow together the stress is on information. Miller, at a later stage under 'Basic Concepts', describes the difference between nonliving and living systems where he states that nonliving systems do not have the characteristics of a living system. Living systems are open systems and they maintain a steady state of negentropy even though entropy changes occur in them as they do everywhere else. When the Earth is depicted as a practically closed living system it is for the reason of seeing the implications when critical subsystems are missing or are incomplete. e.g. extruder, reproducer, decider; and because these subsystems ought to be analysed in order to see in what way their characteristics determine the survival of the Earth. (Extruder is particularly described in *Figures 12:8, 12:9,* and *12:10.*

An organism in balance or steady state can survive as long as the conditions for the critical subsystems are not threatened, but this does not mean that the individual organism avoids an irreversible process because it is described as an open system. In Bunge (1989 p. 357) it is seen as advisable to speak of actions that are mainly, but never totally, constructive. If we are to live we cannot help but increase the environmental entropy, or disorder. Levy (1992 p. 335) maintains

> "the promise of a-life, and the powerful benefits it draws by apparent violation of a different law - the second law of thermodynamics - are as illusory as the belief that life actually does violate the second law; and in the long run an entropic bill is to be paid and further some of these consequences are already apparent: the order we created by building the edifices of our civilization has already resulted in entropy pollution."

There is a contradiction in asserting that a living system, such as an individual organism, is open and that it is at the same time moving towards an equilibrium. Nilsson (1983) has dealt with this question and says that one of the most essential laws of physics basically concerns oblivion. The Entropy Law, the second main proposition of thermodynamics, states that order is continually obliterated and disorder increases. Still Nature has an extraordinary capability of creating information and remembering information; otherwise no genetic inheritance could exist, and no life be possible. Here lies a paradox which, for hundreds of years and more has worrying many people who have philosophizied about Nature. How is it really possible that creation and evolution can be in progress within the Universe? Churchland (1988 p. 188) notes that evidently, the evolution of complex structures is not to be found in a closed system a standpoint which can be seen to be inaccurate when the Earth is regarded as a closed system. The question is whether this also applies to living systems as species and to the biosphere as a living system. The implications of the laws of thermodynamics can be interpreted in such a way that when living systems have been moving towards increasing complexity involving an increase in the number of species, this occurs contemporaneously with an increasing entropy in the whole system which is, in practice closed. We are now experiencing an increase in entropy which is taking place in the Earth as a system (according to the assumptions made here) and which can lead to a decrease in the number of species, at the same time as we are moving towards a state where more and more metabolic waste is produced.

According to Schrödinger (1944) the essential thing in metabolism is that the organism succeeds in freeing itself from all the entropy it produces while alive. But this is not the fact when, at the global level, we see that metabolic waste is increasing. The difference in the rate of increase depends on the extent to which the system is influenced in the two cases (when it is regarded as a closed system or as an "open" living system). When the Earth is regarded as a closed system then it is up to us, living in the system, to see the difference when the increase of entropy threatens steady state, and when there are dissipative structures (which are prerequisites of possibilities for evolution).

Bohm and Peat (1987 p. 189 Swedish ed.) write that they see the possibility of global destruction, which may lay waste the natural order on which all life depends. The following references from the literature perused illustrate the uncertainty which exists concerning how the term can be applied.

Tim Jackson thinks of the Earth as a closed, but not isolated system thermodynamic system in Jackson (1993 p. 6). He also distinguishes between open systems which are open to the interchange of both material and energy with their environment; closed systems which are open to the interchange of energy but which are materially closed; and isolated systems which are closed to the interchange of both energy and matter. According to Conrad (1983) the planet's entire ecosystem is essentially closed.

According to Koide and Abiko, in Mayumi (1991), the Earth, our abode, can be regarded as a big (closed) Carnot engine with the sun (a heat reservoir at a higher temperature) and outer space (a heat reservoir at lower temperature). They declare that meteorite fall, the amount of particles that escape the gravitational field, the amount of heat production by consumption of fossil fuels and the amount of geothermal heat can be ignored in this connection.

Worldwatch Institute 91 (p. 7 Swedish ed.) maintains that the Earth is a system which follows the S-curve which all biological growth follows, and that the ability of the biosphere to neutralize waste from energy systems based on oil will in the long run prove to be a more restricting factor than the deficit of oil. Nearly 6 billion tons of carbon compounds are discharged annually into the air in the form of carbon dioxide, a greenhouse gas which seems to be continually increasing within the atmosphere. The economy works within the boundaries for global ecosystems, with limited possibilities to produce fresh water, produce new top-soil and absorb pollutants. Kenneth E. Boulding is of the same opinion when he in Hopkins (1966 p. 12) says that it seems to be pollution rather than exhaustion which is the primary problem confronting us.

Hershey (1986 p. 6) writes that the real world dictates the transformation, of raw materials or energy, in one direction only: low entropy to high entropy.

A similar view is maintained by Prigogine where he mentions a town and a living cell as examples of dissipative structures that may not be able to produce order out of chaos when restrictions relating to waste are imposed.

Against the background of what Miller (1978) writes under Chapter 5 "Input information overload" it is difficult to draw lines between open and closed systems. A system is open as long as it is able to maintain its steady state, but as soon as the living system, for example as a result of errors (which can arise in the subsystems for a number of reasons), can no longer handle information input, for example, then entropy increases and the system dies. When the incoming information cannot be handled and the number of faults increases the survival of the system will finally be threatened. However, there must be a way of describing the transition from the situation where a system can maintain its steady state and the point where its limit is reached and the system starts to fail. Concerning entropy and GLST, Miller writes (p. 83): "A system's organization at all levels undergoes entropic changes" and "Yet one way or another, sooner or later, all living systems appear finally to terminate. For cells, as for societies, time's arrow points ultimately to the dust of entropy."

This view also corresponds to the one presented in Auger (1989). Eric D. Schneider and James J. Kay have in ISSS meeting (1989) suggested a way to cope with changes in entropy (p. 23):

> "The following is an outline of terms used that require rigorous definitions with relevant mathematical descriptions as well as measurements that can or need to be made for descriptions of time dependent behavior of system evolution. System, equilibrium, gradient, dissipation, degradation, efficiency, effectiveness, stability, entropy, entropy production, specific entropy production, energy, exergy, power, field, force, emergence, evolution, order, organization, complexity, coherent behavior, nonlinear behavior, stress, size, flow structure."

However this last sentence presents a long list of complex concepts to which it is difficult to give mathematical interpretations. Over and above mathematical explanations, when one is obliged to add non-mathematical explanations, as is the case when starting from axioms one reaches a certain amount of complexity. Van Gigch (1974 p. 41)) writes

> "that if open systems are to be regarded as closed systems where the environment is intentionally ignored this involves great risks of misunderstanding. One takes no account of the fact that information processing in living systems reduces positive entropy or of the drawing of energy from the environment (an increase of negative entropy) which counteracts the decaying tendencies of irreversible natural processes (an increase in positive entropy)."

It is possible that there may be some variation in the speed with which entropy increases (depending on the possibility of processing the variables stated) but there is even so no change in the laws of thermodynamics relating to a continuing process which means an increase of entropy in open systems as well, and finally ending in death (equilibrium).

MEASURING ENTROPY

The mass, the amount of energy, can all be measured in units of the metric system. The amount of information can be measured by the Shannon statistic (H), which is the negative of entropy. But for a complete measurement of the processes of living systems, another sort of unit, not yet discovered, is essential according to Miller (1978 p. 1030). The problem of measuring entropy is illustrated by C. Dyke in Weber (1988), where he writes that we measure "costs and benefits" in terms of sacrifices of energy and time in a structure where maximum efficiency is to be achieved. He also says (p. 365): "We never, except in the most superficial ways, examine the relationships between our patterns of social organization and the rate of material flow needed to sustain them. This optimal efficiency is never satisfactorily connected to the time-dependent thermodynamic conditions that really matter."

Bunge (1989) maintains that the environmental issue and its relationship to social development of greater importance than everything except the nuclear arms race. The difficulty of describing the implications of the term entropy also means that changes are hard to measure. Hershey and Lee in

Hersey, Daniel and Lee W. E. III (1987) carried out measurements relating to the increase in entropy in open systems and the results of these show how a living organism continuously increases its entropy and approaches a dangerous state of maximum entropy.

Experts try to approximate such conditions of different kinds e.g. in Worldwhatch Institute 91, Luft'90 (Air '90), IGBP 90, OECD 90 when they measure the global metabolic rate.

One conceivable way of measuring the increase of entropy at the level of the Earth would be to measure the connection between the consumption of fuel and the increase of pollutants that contribute to raising the temperature of the Earth. One might also measure the connections between a reduced life span and the results of metabolic waste which, via air and water, injures plant and animal life.

By analysing the connection indicated between Extruder (at different levels) and the influence on the Earth's conditions, it might be possible to study different subsystems and their connection within the whole system as in the simulation examples.

Experts try to approximate such conditions when they measure the global metabolic rate. One quotation which establishes a connection between the increase of entropy and its relation to time is shown in *Figure 9:2* and following figures which show relations between entropy (time) and systems. What is needed according to Wellburn is a new branch non-equilibrium thermodynamics (NET) where the fluxes can be measured by determining the rate of heat production under conditions in which the systems may be assumed to perform no work other than maintenance work. Weber (1988). Chapter 3 "The Dissipative Ecosystem" Conrad (1983) has a classification of entropy measures under the section "The Chessboard Analogy" where six different entropy concepts: Thermodynamic entropy, Macroscopic diversity (functionally distinct), Macroscopic diversity (functionally equivalent), Behavioral uncertainties, Entropy of organization, and Structural diversity (diversity of components) – are reviewed under conditions of certain limitations of the analogy. One conclusion in the chapter is that the global entropy is increasing which is in agreement with my statement.

Rate of Increase of Entropy

Another way of describing the change of entropy would be to measure the rate of increase in relation to the depletion of the Earth's energy resources. The results of these measurements must be placed in relation to the values that apply in respect of the survival of living systems. The crucial question seems not in the first place to be how long the Earth's resources of raw materials will last, though the problems of measurement are virtually insurmountable. Where individual forms of energy are concerned one might be able to estimate a duration given no change in conditions, that is to say, unchanged technologies, population growth etc. However, this route is beset with the obstacles that are attributed to the fundamental question of the description of the microstates of thermodynamic systems. Weber (1988 p. 146)

> "The basis for assigning a thermodynamic system and entropy comes from the fundamental indeterminability of its microstates. A thermodynamic macrostate cannot be tied down in an arrangement. Entropy is a measure of this lack of "tied-downability". It is a property of the macrostate, of the ensemble of possibilities, rather than of any microstate."

The decisive issue is where the limit for survival goes, this limit describing a macrostate, and how this is related to estimating what rate of increase in production endangers the subsystems especially producer and converter. By means of simulation it is possible to study how the extruder subsystem, which removes waste from the living system, is related to the levels of the cell, the organization and the Earth.

Energy Flows and Entropy

Depew and Weber (1988 p. 260) introduce a view which is in conformity with the figures that show connections between the cell and the Earth and have the entropy arrow underneath. The figures showing the cell-Earth system as a living system are in line with the viewpoint (p. 261) articulated in the following quotation.

> "From this perspective we note once more that natural selection has been reconceived in terms of processes and pattern flows rather than products of

purely competitive relationships. What are selected are differential patterns of energy flows, in which those that are fittest are those that best enhance the autocatalytic behavior of the reward loops in which they participate. In other words, flow patterns are selected because they contribute to the stability and coherence of the whole system of which they are a part."

This is also in conformity with the view of De Duve (1984) and Herrman (1989), who state that pattern flows are selected because they contribute to the stability and coherence of the whole systems of which they are a part, and also with Miller (1978), where we read: "In later stages of ecosystems development this leads to more highly articulated networks of energy flow, wherein those pathways that foster more efficient transfers flourish at the expense of less effective routes." Self-organizing systems arise as a result of what Depew and Weber describe as a flow of energy running through them. Energy comes exclusively from the sun and in that sense systems have an environment. If thereafter, at different levels and as a whole, they seem to have the ability to develop towards a higher degree of complexity then this may be described as a capacity for self-organization. A steady energy flow is combined with a constantly increasing complexity in living systems, but this complexity seems to be counteracted by that energy flow which gives rise to an increasing rate of metabolic waste.

ENTROPY COMPARED WITH ECONOMIC VIEWS

Figure 8:1 below has been taken from Samuelson (1964 p. 181; ed.1985 has the same figure p. 106) and shows one measure of how "Net national product is measured as flow of output as equal flow of costs." The figure describes economic flows (transactions) and assumes equilibrium when investments correspond to savings. It does not show how fast or how great the flows are regarding non-renewable resources or the pollution which results from the economic activities. The flows are determined, in accordance with economic theory, by means of conditions which determine the connection between consumption purchases, goods and services, productive services and wages, interest, profit, etc. A later addition to this figure shows a pump A attached to the "business" rectangle and an investment outflow at Z by the "public" rectangle. The function of the pump is described so that technological change, population growth, and other dynamic factors keep the investment pump handle going. Income rises and falls with changes in investment, its maintainable equilibrium level being realized only when intended saving at Z continues to match intended investment at A.

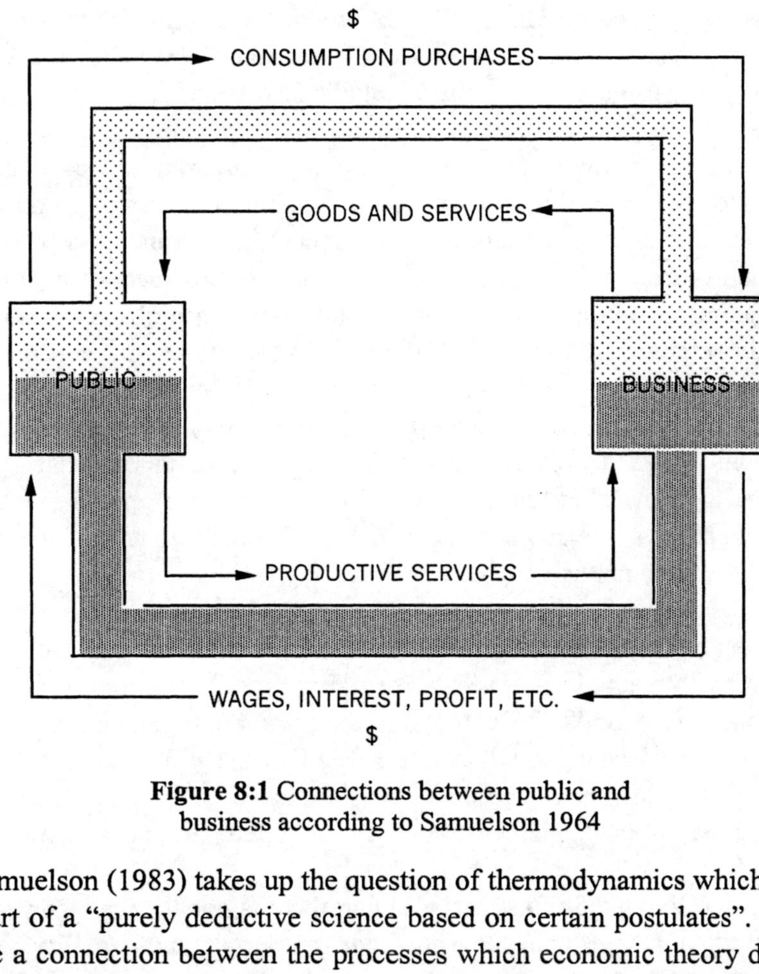

Figure 8:1 Connections between public and business according to Samuelson 1964

Samuelson (1983) takes up the question of thermodynamics which he sees as a part of a "purely deductive science based on certain postulates". He does not see a connection between the processes which economic theory describes and an increase in entropy due to the economic processes. Samuelson gives primacy to points of similarity between certain economic "laws" which functionally correspond to the First and Second Laws of Thermodynamics.

The economic approach in Hardwick (1986), is not basically different from the one adopted by Samuelson and presented in *Figure 8:1*. Hardwick's figure shows that "the environment has a limited assimilative capacity as a waste disposal sink." However, the emphasis is still on an economic presentation of the difference between the social marginal cost and the private marginal cost. It is a difference that is due to the fact that private producers fail to take account of the external (public bads and public goods) marginal cost. The increase in entropy sees no differences between private producers and others, and is dependent on the difference over time between input and output, regardless of administrative form. Hardwick (1989) shows a recycling process where an increase in entropy takes place either as negentropy comes from “environment as a supplier of resources”, “environment as an amenity”, or as the recycling that can take place from “environment as a sink.” A reduced increase in entropy per unit of time could be achieved through using less of “environment as a supplier of resources” and an increase in recycling from “environment as a sink.” Hardwick points to cost-benefit analysis as a way of taking account of all relevant social costs and benefits. This is a part of trying to overcome environmental problems but it has also to conform to the conditions that apply in respect of the survival of the living system.

Using macro-economic theory as a base Radetzki (1990) has analysed connections between growth and environment. He maintains that empirical observations show that environmental qualities are improved when the economy grows and becomes more dense. He says that the “greenhouse gases” so far have not had any discernible effect on the environment. However he says later on that our knowledge of the relations between economic activity and the environment is incomplete, but economic growth and technological progress has enlarged our ability to take care of future environmental catastrophes of all kinds. He also makes the reservation that economic growth and technological changes which are related to the growing global activity may unintentionally destroy essential environmental qualities. One of my aims is to find out if the statements in the first three sentences above can be supported.

Ryding (1992 p. 654) also stresses that there is not always a contradiction between economic growth and satisfactory environmental quality. He sees economic development as a positive force and a necessary condition for environmental protection. He points to the policy response to safeguard the environment and to assure the sustainability of economic growth. Bunge (1989) proposes to adopt what he calls ecosociodevelopment, i.e. integral (not just economic, cultural or political) development together with environmental management.

A fourth source which sees to the connection between the development and the environment is World Development Report (1992) which sees a growing consensus that policies for economic efficiency and for environmental management are complementary. The report maintains that development versus the environment is a false dichotomy when the benefits from rising incomes are offset by the costs imposed on health and quality of life by pollution. It cannot be called development when environmental damage can undermine future productivity.

Charles A. S. Hall (1990 p. 123) says that in the U. S. economics is taught as a social science and focuses on the needs and wants of people as they express them in the marketplace.

> "But as a social science, economics normally ignores or treats as irrelevant the physical characteristics of resources, except as they are reflected in prices, and it is less interested in empirical validation, for that is difficult in most social sciences. This approach causes severe flaws in how people perceive the resource base that must underlie any real economic activity."

Hall goes on later to say that the models would be constrained by laws of thermodynamics and mass balance.

Georgescu-Roegen (1971) maintains that the economic process materially consists of a transformation of low entropy into high entropy, i.e. into waste, and that this process is irrevocable.

Nagel (1961) writes that he is critical of economic theory because the differences between the idealized conditions that are presumed to apply for economic laws and reality are so great that the value of the theory can be questioned. Further criticism is made in Boulding (1978) where he sees the irreversibility of the processes that take place according to the second law of thermodynamics.

When the development of society is "steered" according to an idea illustrated by the cycle in *Figure 8:1*, with no account taken of its relationship to the increase in entropy, this is one of the contributory causes of the global deterioration of our environment. This is due to the fact that the necessary tools for considering the overall picture of the flow and degradation of energy in human society — the metabolism of the social organism, its primary function of self-maintenance — have been available for only a short time, a fact which also C. Dyke points out in Weber (1988). The following quotations (p. 365) can be linked with *Figure 8:1*:

> "without a gradient down which material flow can cascade, no dissipative structure can remain stable. Genuine economic equilibrium looms as the heat death of our civilization." and (p. 356)
> "much of classical, neo-classical, orthodox economic theory — in fact — makes use of techniques that play down or obscure the essential time dependence of economic processes."

This aspect of time-dependence is also emphasized in Georgescu-Roegen (1971 p. 245) and (p. 72) where he quotes Whitehead who maintained that no science can "claim to be founded upon observation" if it insists that the ultimate facts of nature "are to be found at durationless instants of time."

The huge extent and the rapid growth of the world's economy, about 20 trillion dollars, has been seen as a great success according to World Watch Institute (1991). But looking beoynd this, as the destruction of the environment increases, the consequences of the failure to close the gap between the economic systems and the natural systems become all too evident. Further criticism of the way economists work without considering the geophysical and biological sciences is made by Eriksson (1987), who points out that economic processes in society always involve matter, energy, entropy, and information, and that economists work without any basic knowledge of thermodynamics and information theory.

A statement of almost the same purport is put forward in Constanza (1991) by the authors Robert Constanza, Herman E. Daly and Joy A. Bartholomew. They see computer simulations as one of our best tools for helping us understand complex functions of integrated ecological economic systems. They list (p. 13) a number of (13) major research questions. This work they have done in order to give examples and suggestions for answering them. Two of the questions are: "What are appropriate model structures for a range of urban, agricultural, and natural subsystems, at several hierarchical scales?" and "How can we develop a philosophy of modelling which is open to the emergence of novelty and consistent with evolutionary, dynamic, whole systems, and multiscale paradigm?"

Kenneth E. Boulding and Herman E. Daly also in Constanza (1991) deal with the relationships between the economic and ecological subsystems. They point out the danger of seeing the macro economy as a system unconstrained by mass balance, entropy, and finitude. In Hopkins (1966 p. 4) Boulding mentions that economists in particular, for the most part, have failed to come to grips with the ultimate consequences of the transition from the open to the closed Earth.

For this reason it is necessary under *Figure 8:1* as well as under *Figure 1:2* and following figures which illustrate the living system, to insert an arrow showing that the system is moving towards increasing entropy. *Figure 8:1* shows changes in GNP which, even if not explicitly put, easily lead to the conclusion that the rate of increase in GNP provides the basis for increased prosperity. The costs involved in cleaning up after oil catastrophes then contribute towards an increase in GNP. In Sweden it has been decided (1990) that, from GNP calculated on the basis of earlier methods of calculating, the costs involved in combating the factors that adversely affect the environment are to be deducted.

World Development Report (1992 p. 4) focuses on three problems arising from environmental problems: human health may be harmed, economic productivity may be reduced, and the pleasure or satisfaction obtained from an unspoiled environment, often referred to as its "amenity" value, may be lost. All are difficult to measure, but the third is especially so. UN has made an investigation of living conditions throughout the world based on other than economic viewpoints. This shows that the ranking list of countries which, on the basis of GNP, have the highest living standards would have to be changed if a different standard based on other variables were to be applied. According to the UN report the economic standard is not the sole determinant when it comes to assessing the standard of living, since this also involves the question of quality of life.

ENTROPY AND BIOLOGICAL ORDER

As was noted earlier, in *Figures 1:2*, the increase in entropy will set a limit for the evolution of biological order and the survival of the living system. What now remains to be seen is at what point the increase in entropy places this limit and how fast the increase takes place. The limit will be reached at different points of time for different parts of the ecosystem.

The attempt to describe living systems using GLST, where the living system is moving toward increasing entropy, is supported by the following passage from Herrman (1989 p. 877) where "the possibility has been considered that the evolutionary increase in structural complexity and complexity of information content has occurred concomitantly with an increase in entropy. In view of criticism of this approach a revaluation of the nature of entropy in thermodynamics, in information theory, and in evolution was attempted." It may also be possible to observe a connection between matter-energy consumption incurred when producing housing and industrial products and pollutants.

What we now see may indicate the possibility that biological order can spontaneously increase locally at the expense of increased entropy in the whole system. The evolution of systems (society and supranational system) near the level of the Earth occurs concomitantly with increasing complexity, and they are affected by metabolic waste which is produced at lower levels. In Sweden's Technical Attache´s report (1989) it emerges that one of the major problems is the shortage of land (at the level of the society), which means that it has been necessary to drastically reduce dumping as well as waste production. In the section "simulation" the increase in entropy might be indicated by measuring the relationship between energy consumption and the quantity of energy supplied, and linking this to the quantity of waste products. The simulation shows how the extruder subsystem at different levels can describe these relationships *Figure 12:11*. The system will find it increasingly difficult to distinguish the negentropy necessary for its survival from the increasing entropy in the environment.

Entropy and the Life Length of Living Systems

When the system moves in the direction of increasing entropy according to the Second Law of Thermodynamics the processes in the structure of the living system are affected. The question is how they are affected. Are the conditions of survival determined by conditions that are primarily dependent on the laws of thermodynamics? Is the length of life primarily determined by how matter-energy and information flows between subsystems or other factors? Examples of such factors are given in Bailey (1990 p. 83):"Entropy is the opposite of information" in O. Klapp's formulation. Thus, one source of entropy is information overload. Other examples of entropy that may be communicated into systems are "noise", "banality", "boringness of signals", "restriction. and lack of reinforcement".

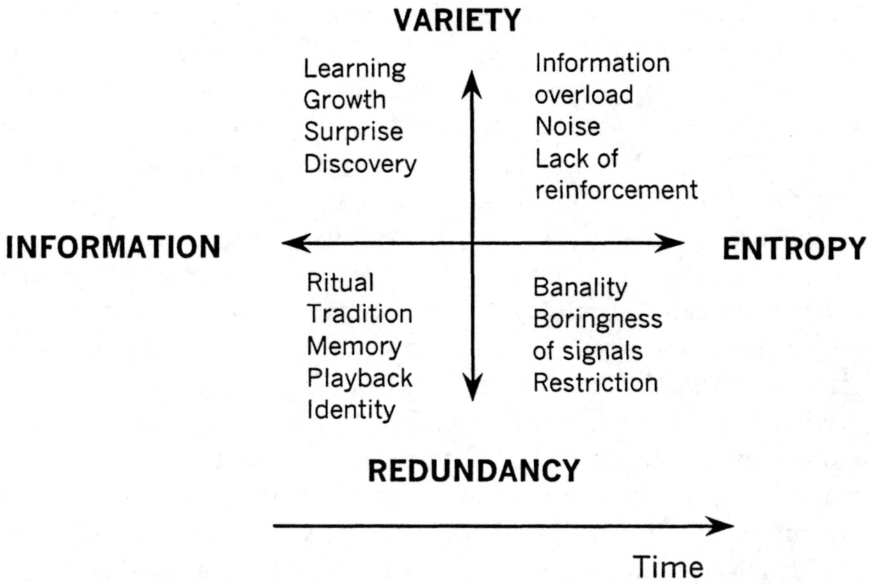

Figure 8:2 (the figure is here turned so that the entropy axis point along the x-axis) is taken from Klapp's report "Opening and Closing in Open Systems" Klapp 1976. A time arrow has also been added.

Klapp (1976) maintains that apart from the entropy developed within the system there can also be an increase in entropy as a result of the importation of external entropy.

In Miller (1978) in the chapter describing information input overload (pp. 121-202) the curves that describe the relationships between input information and output in bits per second rise to a certain limit which is different for different systems (p. 192). For a cell maximum output is shown as being around 5 000 bits per second when input is around 90 000 bits per second, after which the curves flatten out (for the organism output is shown as 8 bits per second with an input of 10 bits per second). However, Miller has not indicated if or where a limit exists when information input is so great that the system ceases to produce any output. If and when this limit is reached or in close proximity to it one ought to be able to describe a system as closed. Miller writes that losses in the form of entropy can come about in the processes that take place in the memory subsystem 3.3.6. Is the scale of these losses independent of the period of time for which, for example, a cell is subjected to a high input of bits per second?

In principle, the curves that describe information input overload ought also to be able to describe the matter-energy input overload relationship. The system will not be able to consume an unlimited or injurious (e.g. polluted) matter-energy input and will in the end approach a state where it can no longer be regarded as open. These questions bring us close to a cross-level analysis of extruder in the section on simulation.

Bailey (Bailey 1990 p. 81) considers Prigogine's equation for open (living) systems: dS = deS+diS, where dS is the total increase in entropy in the system deS is the external entropy increase put into the system, and diS is the internal increase in entropy due to irreversible processes in the system. If diS is constant or increases (dS is greater than or equal to zero) then deS can be negative if sufficient quantities of matter-energy are put into the system, and the total entropy of the system can thereby be reduced. However, there is a danger that deS and diS are regarded as directly comparable quantities. diS may to some extent consist of metabolic waste (and the factors that Klapp lists above) which the system cannot get rid of and which threaten it. Klapp sees in (1973 p. 13-16) the survival of people (an organism) as well as a society as being threatened when there is too much and when the need for balance of opening and closure is not recognized. With regard to a group he says (p. 156): "Any group has a range of tolerance to entropy, but beyond a point (which may be different for each group) increase in entropy leads to a crisis in collective identity, often called anomie. Beyond that range, entropy becomes irreversible: "we" breaks down, alienation increases with resulting loss of morale and membership, and the group is likely to break up. The question then is whether one can agree with Bailey's statement: "Since virtually all social and biological systems are regarded as open." As I see it, we should be more inclined to regard them as semiclosed, as Churchland does, in contrast also to Miller who regards living systems and the Earth as open systems.

Emery (1969) says that the total change of entropy in an open system can be negative as well as positive — that although the second law is not violated, or more precisely, it holds for the system plus its environment, although it does not hold for the system itself. This is also in accordance with my statement that when the Earth cannot dispose of all of its waste to an environment it has to be seen as a closed system.

It is also opposite in contrast to what is said in Penrose (1989 p. 413): "What the earth does, is to take energy in a low-entropy form, and spew it all back again into space, but in a high-entropy form." In Figure 7.7 (p. 414) he shows how the earth takes in few high-energy photons and sends many low-energy photons back into space. It seems to run contrary to what he also says (p. 412), that "We take in energy in a low–entropy form (food and oxygen) and we discard it in a high-entropy form (heat, carbon dioxide, excreta)" when we are in fact facing a situation with an increasing world temperature and an increasing amount of excreta. The pollution of the atmosphere also has the consequence that the ozone layer is damaged, meaning that plants and animals are affected by an increasing amount of UV light. As a consequence they are, in addition to the greenhouse effect, affected by an increasing entropy.

ALTERNATIVE INTERPRETATIONS OF THE CONCEPT OF ENTROPY

In an article (1998) "Thermodynamics, Information and Life Revisited, Part 1: 'To Be or Entropy' in Systems Research? Peter A. Corning's and Stephen Jay Kline's, write about the meaning of the concept of entropy (p. 275)

> "we will begin by drawing a critically important distinction between physical 'order' of various kinds and the 'functional organization' that characterizes living systems. We will then outline what we believe is the appropriate paradigm for theorizing about the role of energy and information in biological processes. In essence, our paradigm is cybernetic."

Corning's and Kline's article is long and very illuminating in its account of different points of view of the concept of entropy, but I am not quite sure how their view can be understood and applied to my understanding of living systems. They depict (p. 289)

> "the costs for living organisms of capturing and using various forms of available energy, along with the relative efficiency and 'profitability' of those transactions and the ancillary and theoretically subordinate problems associated with disposing of wasted and degraded energy from irreversible thermodynamic processes (the 'externalities' in economics terminology)". Clausius is quoted who in "Abhandlungen über die mechanische Wärmetheorie (1864) wrote "The energy of the universe is constant; the entropy of the universe tends towards a maximum (quoted in Harold, 1986). Clausius also coined the term 'heat death'".

Corning and Kline say that "the dour vision of Clausius" has long since become the conventional wisdom of the Western scientific establishment", where they among others mention von Bertalanffy and Miller.

Miller (Living Systems 1978) mentions entropy in several contexts; on (p. 13) he says "The disorder, disorganization, lack of patterning, or randomness of organization of a system is known as its entropy (S). He also sees (p. 13) three sorts of evidence which suggests relationships between information and entropy. On (p. 16) is a table where the "relationships of information and entropy" are shown. The table is headed Information (H) versus Entropy (–S)

H	=	**–S**
Information		Uncertainty
Negentropy		Entropy
Signal		Noise
Accuracy		Error
Regularity		Randomness
Pattern or form		Lack of pattern or formlessnes
Order		Disorder
Organization		Disorganization
Regular complexity		Irregular simplicity
Heterogenity		Homogenity
Improbability (Only one alternative correctly describes the form)		Probability (More than one alternative correctly describes the form)
Predictability (Only one alternative correctly describes the form)		Unpredictability (More than one alternative correctly describes the form)

On (p. 43) Miller says that "Transmission or storage of information is associated with the temporary existence of the system in a state of lower entropy. The decrease of entropy can be taken as a measure of the amount of information." Corning and Kline do not seem to agree with the view of Schrödinger (p. 18) "What an organization feeds upon is negative entropy".

Miller refers to Ilya Prigogine (p. 35) and says, regarding open systems, "it is possible for entropy not to increase in such systems, and they are able to maintain steady states." But Miller also says (p. 18) of living systems "They maintain a steady state of negentropy even though entropic changes occur in them as they do everywhere else. Murray Gell-Mann (The Quark and the Jaguar p. 262 Swedish edition 1997) maintains also that entropy and information are very close related. In fact entropy can be seen as a measure of ignorance.

CONCLUSION

According to the different interpretations in the preceding quotations there are different meanings of the concept entropy: Those which are related to information, to flows of energy and to a probability for a state. Until more general agreement is reached as to how the concept of entropy is to be interpreted I maintain the view which shows increasing entropy in a practically closed system, as is shown in *Figure 1:2*.

Chapter 9

CYBERNETICS

INTRODUCTION

According to my earlier experience systems at different levels in living systems ought to be depicted in a manner which permits studies of changes between and within levels. It is then necessary to code subsystems and parameters in a uniform way, in this case on the basis of codes and symbols depicted in Living Systems. References in literature and statistics relating to the model should be accesssible within the model so that it should not be necessary to go outside the model in order to get access to the bases of the information sources. When the information foundation of the model is easily accessible on the Internet this will facilitate the possibility of studying and comparing alternative sources in order to see in what way they can influence the result of the simulation. I have in the following included three *Figures 9:4, 9:5,* and *9:6,* from my thesis which illustrate different aspects of the concept of the cybernetic process; I have also given examples of how it can be interpreted and depicted

Here I would like to draw attention to the time factor, which can have decisive importance. A system which becomes exposed to influence from the environment perhaps does not react before a certain amount of time has passed. This can especially occur at the higher levels but of course also at the lower levels, such as organ and cell. A disease does not perhaps develop until years after the impact has taken place. It is also important to study the general problem of how cause and effect can be seen and explained (philosophically or otherwise). Cyclical changes which occur over time in many systems and belong to one of the system's qualities are another problem which may be difficult to separate from the actual impacts.

THE CELL – THE EARTH SYSTEM

In the introduction to his book De Duve (1984 p. 1) (A Guided Tour of the Living Cell) emphasises that: "When we speak of the living cell as the object of our tour, we mean some sort of common denominator of all living cells that shares with them the main attributes of life." In Aulin (1989) he points to problems in the World III model that was created by the "Club of Rome", and notes the absence of a "rationally" based view of society and social developments as a basis for scientific research resting on a "model-construction strategy". Aurelio Peccei (managing director of the Club of Rome) and Daisaku Ikeda have however in Pecci (1984) pointed out, adopting a more comprehensive view, the need for a new line of policy which presupposes an understanding what our objectives and goals are and assumes that we try to achieve them. If the Earth is to be seen as the highest level, then a system at global level has to be created (which in itself would embrace several supranational systems) which views the Earth as a whole as its sphere of responsibility. It can seem that we are far from obtaining a unit able to take decisions at this level, though work has started in a number of areas such as the World Wide Fund for Nature, the IMF, WHO and UN.

INFORMATION AND COMMUNICATION SYSTEMS

One of the reasons for seeing the Earth as the ninth level is for example that a number of 251 stationary satellites now orbiting the Earth may be regarded as a "component" in the Earth's channel and network. By means of the information flows, subsystems at different levels can be supplied with information about the Earth's weather, about preparations for warfare, about the spread of the deserts and the contraction of rain forests, as well as about cartography — to mention just a few possibilities. Communication technology provides the means of transferring, without loss of time, information in the model at the global level, which contains information-processing subsystems (input transducers, internal transducers, channel and networks, decoders, associators, memory, deciders, encoders and output transducers) in the same way as at the other levels.

One person who points to the importance of regarding the Earth as a level is Stafford Beer in his Banquet Address to the Silver Jubilee Meeting on Operational Research and the Social Sciences, Queen's College, Cambridge, April 12, 1989. Beer writes in Systems Practice (1989 p. 282)–"We move towards a global level of recursion. The nation states do not work any more as the world contracts — and is more and more threatened." He continues "A world government is imperative" and "people belong to this planet, and the planet belongs to them — as long as we do not wreck its amazing power of self-repair." GLST indicates the importance of data flows; as Beer points out, what we require is (p. 283) "the sophisticated filtration of data flows in real time to detect that instability and, thereby, to prevent disasters before they occur", which is in line with the conditions for the survival of a living system. Miller (1978 p. 903) notes that mutual dependency, exchange of matter-energy and information, and joint decision-making may confer many system characteristics on international relationships. If a superordinate decider is not in control, there is no concrete supranational system, or the ninth system that is proposed here.

It is of interest to note that similar ideas are put forward in De Duve (1984 p. 277), who writes concerning cell biology under the heading "Where Is the Boss?" Different cells are different essentially because they have different complements of proteins and when such cells associate to form an organism, a network of networks of interactions is produced. "In turn, as organisms join into groups, societies, ecosystems, up to the whole biosphere, networks of higher and higher order are built up, finally to embrace, in a single interwoven unit of incredible complexity, the thin pellicle of living matter that covers our planet." De Duve sees levels as necessary in order to understand the whole and sees the whole as a living system. This is in agreement with the view held by Herrman, also a cell biologist, who looks closely at this question Herrman (1989).

When we realize that we affect the Earth in an unmoniterable way we can be afflicted by paralysis as a result of the information that reaches us from this "incredible complexity". The systems at the different levels will then be unable to receive, process and transmit the information, and the whole system will be subjected to information input overload. One of the important preconditions for avoiding a situation in which input information overload threatens the system as a whole is that the information flow take place freely between and within levels.

As early as in 1970, Sir Geoffrey Vickers (1970 p. 123), warned us about this situation - "for it is indeed true that we created an ungovernable world, in which natural order and man-made order are blended as never before into a system which can be neither interpreted by natural nor governed by man-made laws."

In the context of the ten-year research programme Global Change (1990) the science academies of the world are at present co-operating on these issues within the framework of the International Geosphere Biosphere Programme. Remote analysis via satellites and the establishment of highly-developed computer based information systems are necessary in support of the research programme. The technology used in these fields is developing rapidly.

SURVEY

Miller (1978) depicts cybernetics as the study of methods of feedback control, and underlines that it is an important part of systems theory. Krippendorff, version 2/2/86 (p. 20) "A Dictionary of Cybernetics" sees that nearly all cybernetic theories involve process and change, from the notion of information, as the difference between two states of uncertainty, to theories of adaptation, evolution and growth processes. De Duve (1984) writes that "the cell is a cybernetic system. And so, through its superimposed network of cell-cell interactions, is the organism. In other words, nucleus and cytoplasm do no more than interact with each other in reciprocally co-ordinated fashion." Herrman (1989) also sees the cell as an information system that is part of the cybernetic process.

Wiener (1954), maintains that the last few centuries have been a period of rapid changes that has no parallel in history, and that this is in part a result of more opportunities for communication. He also notes the drawbacks that have accompanied this development. (p. 46):

> "This is partly the result of increased communication, but also of an increased mastery over nature which, on a limited planet like the earth, may prove in the long run to be an increased slavery to nature. For the more we get out of the world the less we leave, and in the long run we shall have to pay our debts at a time that may be very inconvenient for our own survival."

Second–order cybernetics is characterized by the notion of participation. The observer is a participant, interacting with the system. Pask sees this shift as an evolutionary shift, (which among others builds on Ashby and Shannon), rather than a revolutionary change. The upper part of *Figure 9:2* shows in principle Miller's (1978 Figure 1-2 p. 4) with lines that symbolize communication between the critical subsystems at the different levels. If a critical subsystem is absent then its process can be dispersed to a higher or lower level or laterally. The lower part of the figure, with its flows of matter-energy and information, shows the feedback processes that take place from the cell to the Earth and vice versa.

The division into levels undertaken by Miller does not imply a definitive limited division into eight levels. In this section on cybernetics examples are given of how the cell-organism levels may be viewed as a continuum in a manner similar to Figure 1.2 in Vandervert (1990) and also to Bohm & Peat (1987) (p. 108 and 165 in the Swedish edition 1990).

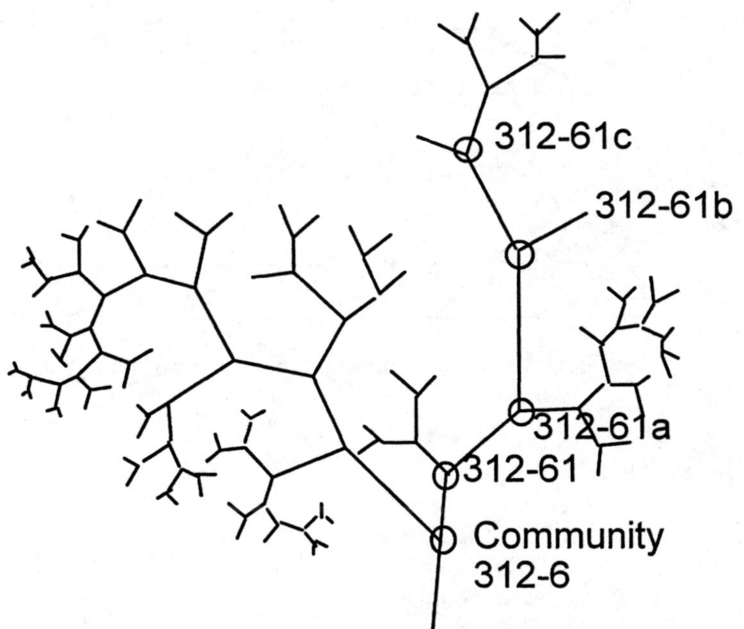

Figure 9:1 (boundary 312-61) is built up hierarchically like the upper part of Figure 9:2 which is based on Figure 1-2 in Miller 1978.

At each dividing line the system can be analysed to lower levels through the 20 critical subsystems at each subsystem level 312-61a a, 312-61b, and 312-6c, with a retention of the connection to the system as a whole.

312-61a refers to *Figure 12:12* which shows an example of subsystems of boundary with a number of components. 312-61b refers to *Figure 12:13* and 312-61c to *Figure 12:14.* In principle this means that the analysis of a system is not confined to nine levels. It can take place with a continuous transition from the highest level to the lowest. *Figure 19* shows an overview of the interactions between 312-61a, 312-61b, and 312-61c and the system.

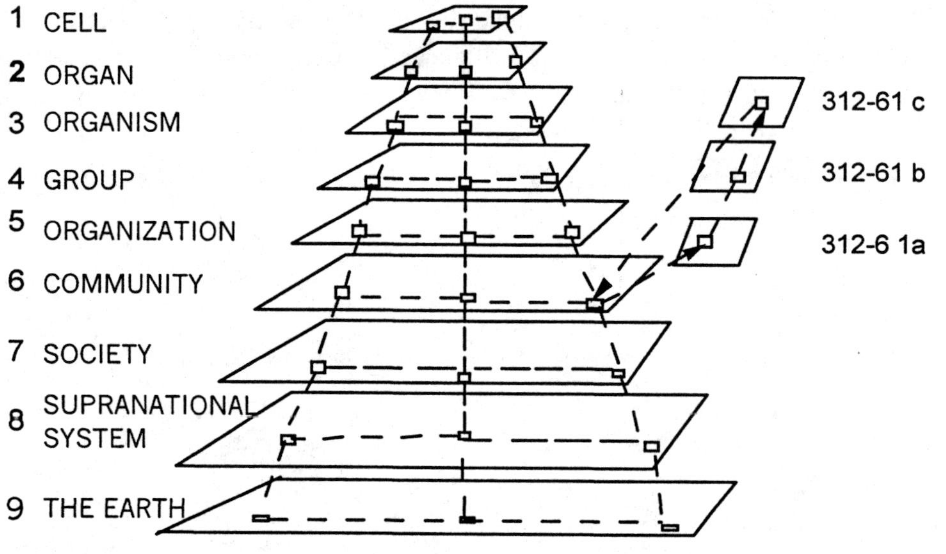

Figure 9:2 Feedback lines shown between subsystems of boundary and extruder. Based on Frandberg 1986.

The Feedback Process

Figure 9:3 is taken from Optner (1965) and shows a cybernetic process with negative feedback loops which accounts for the steering in relation to objectives and goals.

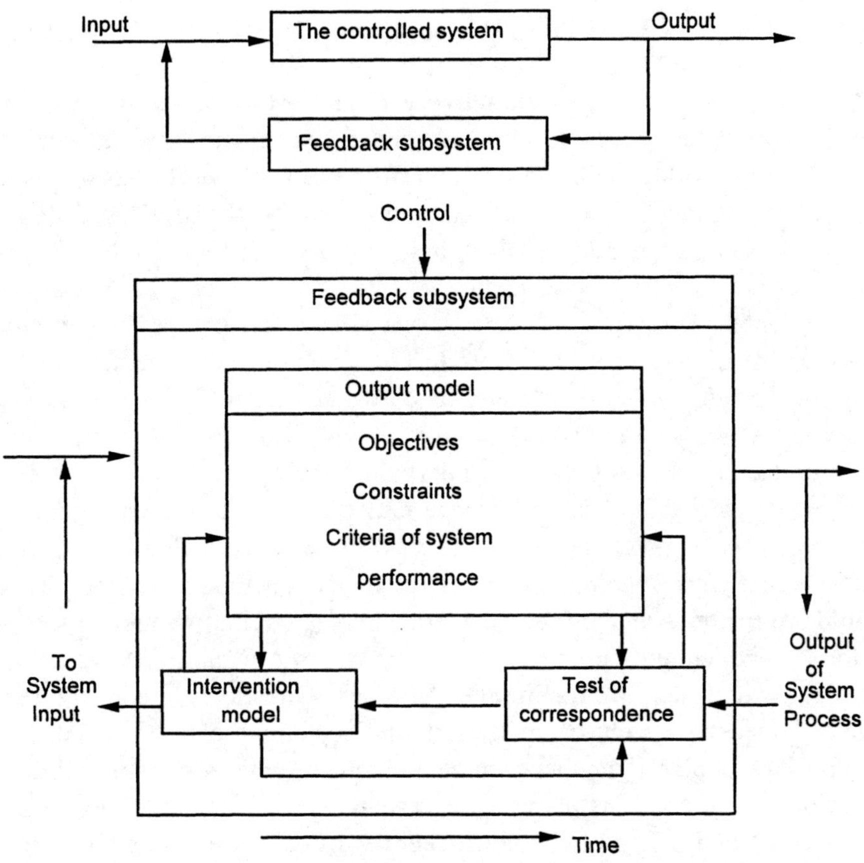

Figure 9:3 Basic properties of a feedback process according to Optner 1965. An arrow depicting time has been added here.

The process gives in principle a basic description and indicates not an observer outside the system but one who is a part of it. A time axis is also added to Optner's figure. Samuelson (1978 Figure 10.1.1) compares the result of an action over a length of time as regards the stored information, information concerning the object system when decisions are made, and decisions which are made in accordance with ultimate objectives and goals and with the guidance of the diagnosis provided, which suggests a certain procedure of action.

Qualitative Connections

The question of how the qualitative variables are to be described is even more difficult than seeing the connections between quantifiable variables. Miller (1978) (p. 500) writes: "One fault of the research on organisms is that studies of effect, emotion, anxiety, motivation, and personality variables have been poorly controlled and usually unquantitative. General Living Systems Theory has not handled these phenomena too well either." How can more precise scientific analyses be made of variables related to effect, emotion, anxiety, motivation, and personality? In his concluding commentary to "The World System" Jay W. Forrester says much the same as Miller when he writes "we have a range of choice in the combination of physical, social, psychological, and moral pressures under which we will live."

The discussion about the difference between quantitative and qualitative methods has been taken up in Kvale (1989), where he does not see any opposition between quantitative versus qualitative methods. He does not see quantitative methods as hard tough-minded versus qualitative methods as soft and loose. The simulation of living systems does not enable us to see in the first place which are the qualitative variables. One notes the result that a suggested measure produces in the simulation, and the effect of different measures can be placed against each other. This provides a starting point for a discussion of the qualities between representatives of different subject areas and interest trends. One of the consequences of this communication is, that people can have access to the information they desire at the right time and at little cost, so as to be able to influence their situation. This is done in order to meet the demands made by a pluralist society. Ulrich (1983) writes that no systems approach for handling real-world complexity can be rational unless it makes room for the (self)-critical reflection of free citizens; for these alone know what social reality is and what it ought to be like. If the last remark is indeed the case then it would seem that allowing "the free citizens" to have their say is a matter of some urgency. This is one of the main purposes here — to facilitate communication and understanding of living systems.

SECOND-ORDER CYBERNETICS

An account of differences between different definitions of second-order cybernetics is given by Umpleby (1990) (p. 113) in the table below.

	First-order cybernetics	Second-order cybernetics
von Foerster	The cybernetics of observed systems	The cybernetics of observing systems
Pask	The purpose of a model	The purpose of a modeller
Varela	Controlled systems	Autonomous systems
	Interaction among the variables in a system	Interaction between observer and observer
Umpleby	Theories of social systems ideas and society	Theories of the interaction between

The properties posited above as characterizing second-order cybernetics seem to be able to be transformed so that they represent first-order cybernetics. The difference between controlled and autonomous systems can change and at the same time the difference between a controlled system and an autonomous one is blurred not least at the level of society. When the levels at particle subatomic level are studied in physics this difference does not exist because observed systems are affected by observing systems. In principle this interconnection occurs between the fourth pair of alternatives put forward by Umpleby. The approach to cybernetics in GLST is based on the process that takes place in feedback transfer in living systems at the levels of the cell – the Earth. GLST sees the whole system and thus the difference between first-order and second-order cybernetics does not arise. The question of the difference between first-order and second-order is similar to the problems where hard systems are characterized by a structure that can be more easily described and influenced than is the case with soft systems, and reflects problems in human society, where, inter alia, Ulrich's criticism is directed at a classification of those who influence and those who are influenced.

Conclusion

The distinctions which are made between first-order cybernetics and second-order cybernetics are based on a distinction between the object, which is observed, and the subject, which observes. However, order is dependent on more than a statement of order by the subject or the object and a relation between them. Order is beyond, it is to be found in both of them. It is a dynamic process which encompasses subject and object and the cycle of perception and communication which unite them and join them in a relation to each other. This implies that the possibility of attaining an order which leads to a coherent and consistent action is always restricted.

DIFFERENT APPROACHES TO THE CYBERNETIC PROCESS

Ulrich defines "rational" planning" as "an effective tool". "A tool" of this kind cannot be "effective" if there is no feedback process, something he has not taken into account in Ulrich (1983 Figure 14.1) which shows the processes leading to "rational planning" contains many statements (categorizations) about what is effective and rational, and gives the impression that it has been written with a "normative content" that is characterized to a large extent by the viewpoint which he opposes so vigorously. He defines his theory as follows: "a constitution theory of experience is, I believe, possible today only by way of a heuristic approach" and adds: "The categories a heuristic approach might yield cannot of course be justified theoretically (i.e. by demonstrating their necessity) but only heuristically, i.e. by referring to their empirically contingent usefulness." How can experience of a measure prove to have "empirically contingent usefulness" if one does not have an understanding of how the feedback process takes place within the viewpoint one applies to the environment, or if one cannot support oneself with quantitative or qualitative information? In his book Ulrich criticizes Beer's way of using his cybernetic thinking with regard to the situation in Chile. He emphasizes the importance of taking account of "deception in the theoretical cybernetic tools". As long as the tools are regarded as scientific and neutral they cannot contribute to social and democratic progress. Here Ulrich brings in the concept of democratic progress without defining either of the words. My intention is not to use GLST as a means of denying that the pluralistic society has advantages; what I am concerned with is how we are to arrive at the decisions that promote the existence and development of society on the basis of the conditions for the living system.

CYBERNETIC MODELS

The criticism that Ulrich directs at the cybernetic view found in Beer applies also in principle to a "Contemporary cybernetic paradigm" and is described as "biological", "organic system", often with the brain as the model; similarly it applies to the criteria for "systems rationality" described according to Ashby's "Law of Requisite Variety". Ulrich misses the target when he describes the dangers of studying wholeness since he in Ulrich (1983 p. 332) writes:

> "As a guide to critically normative reflection on the sources of practical irrationality in cybernetic's organic systems concept (and the syntactic and reductionistic fallacies linked to it), we shall establish the following regulative principle: *In real-world problem solving and design, purposiveness (of tools) depends on purposefulness (of people using tools)"*

His problem-solving perspective is tool design. The implied design ideal is viability in view of external determined pertuberations and purposes. The implied concepts of control are intrinsic and extrinsic –"organic control" and the implied concepts of motivation are extrinsic. A central assumption that Ulrich makes is that social systems are constituted by subjects, not merely by functional organs. Social systems cannot be described only from the starting point of individual "subjects". An understanding of the interactions in society between subjects and between subjects and society is a complex interaction. A subject does not fully exist if it is not living within a society and in accordance with its conditions. In Kvale (1989) Maria Salner writes (p. 48) after having illustrated practices as constituting society or culture:

> "Nor are these social practices reducible to the individual subjective experiences of the human beings that make up a society or a cultural group. The practices themselves have a life of their own, so to speak, because they are collectively created over time, and as a result, they transcend the capacity of any single individual to shape them."

CYCLES

The feedback process is complicated still more because of the impact of cycles of different kinds, and their connection with fluctuations in matter-energy and information. Thompson and Stewart (1986) supply (p. 15-25) examples of "linear and nonlinear oscillations" under various assumptions concerning the preconditions in the initial situation. The examples refer to physical experiments. No more than minor changes to the equations which in the initial situation determine the process of the system can lead to major changes in the appearance of oscillations. The intention here is not to go into all the initial alternatives they demonstrate and which, in the initial situation, affect the appearance of the curves that describe the changes over time.

The relatively simple physical courses of events which can be expressed in mathematical equations, and steer the appearance of "oscillations", give cause for thought when one studies the connection between factors whose connections are described by means of quantifications where the values in many cases cannot be indicated except within large confidence intervals. They write (p. 2) that chaos is likely to occur commonly in non-linear dynamics. Nicolis (1991) has a similar opinion. White (1989 p. 252) writes on "Structural Evolution in Urban Systems" that it is almost a certainty that chaotic dynamic behavior will appear in urban and economic systems and concludes: "Thus indeterminacy is likely to be an important system quality, enabling a system to maintain its own ability to evolve. If that is the case, then any good explanatory model must be able to predict this unpredictability."

In an article in Hall (1992) (p. 88) "The Chaotic Rythms of Life" Robert May, on the basis of results obtained from research on fluctuations in insect populations, points to the difficulties in revealing a discernible signal of what cause the differences in population size. May stresses the fact that the basic problem is "that once patchiness in distribution, environmental noise, and chaotic dynamics all interweave, it can be difficult to disentangle the chaotic, density-dependent signals from additive noise."

Business Cycles

Estey (1964) gives examples of how variations appear over time. The causes of the changes are here explained on the basis of economic theories and "psychological causes". It is of interest to note whether knowledge of business cycles can be transferred to an examination of how these cycles affect changes in matter-energy and information flows in subsystems. Estey stresses (1964 p. 207) that no explanation of the business cycle can be regarded as adequate that does not account for the fact that the production of capital goods fluctuates so much more violently than the production of consumption goods. Wellburn (1988) writes (p. 221):

> "Even if critical comparisons were to be undertaken, the problem of distinguishing the significant from the "background noise" still remains. If it were hypothetically possible to accomplish this, the suspicion is ever present that the answer will never come in a clearcut manner favouring one hypothesis over all the others, but most likely as an interacting combination of many of the components of the various hypotheses already described."

Dewey (1985) proceeds from other causes of the regularities he has been able to indicate in many fields. They may have causes that are due to factors such as for example regular variations in the weather that lie behind variations in crop yields, and which in turn affect a number of factors that can be linked to economic and political decisions. Odum similarly sees connections between the impact of the weather and climate on energy flows and crop yields which in turn steer economic conditions. These explanations (such as the sunspot theory kind) of cyclical changes are not, however, generally accepted in economic theory.

Cyclical Changes in Living Systems

Living systems undergo changes that vary cyclically. A number of these can be observed which apply, for example, to periods between sleep and wakefulness, the level of attention, activities in the nervous system etc. Living systems provide examples of cyclical flows as a result of many interacting factors. It is important to try to see what cyclical changes are characteristic of the initial situation and to try to distinguish these from the changes it is proposed to study by means of simulation. The study of cycles where the importance of the different time which characterize the processes, ranging from milliseconds to years, has been dealt with in Rose (1988). The underlying reasons for the changes in systems that often occur in different kinds of wave like changes are analysed on the assumption that these in principle arise due to interaction between the phenomena that are studied and described. In the initial phase the appearance of the curves in each subsystem described may seem to have been determined by factors that are not made clear. It is possible that one variable in itself has a different 'rhythm' from the rest.

STRUCTURES AND PROCESSES

Cybernetics is linked to the description of the structures and processes of the system. How are we to describe structures and processes in the information-processing subsystems? How are these linked to subsystems that handle matter-energy? What does the channel capacity in the information system look like? How is the steering at different levels linked to goals at different levels? The way simulation of the cell – Earth model is undertaken here in accordance with GLST takes account of the study of the cybernetic process from cell to Earth, taking into consideration the questions listed above. A system at one level cannot survive if one of the properties of a critical subsystem is absent at that level or cannot be transferred to a higher, lower or lateral level. In principle this means that all levels from cell to Earth will be threatened if man (at the organism level) is adversely affected, for example, by input information overload; this will in time affect the whole system. Each level in the hierarchy will in this way be critical for the survival of the whole system. When society suffers from information input overload people (the level of organism), too, will suffer. For this reason it is necessary to study the cybernetic process between the levels from cell to Earth where the vertical lines have been drawn in *Figure 12:7*.

Reference has been made to critics who do not regard such an approach as fruitful, but put their faith in the characteristics of the pluralistic society. We cannot fix rational or scientifically described limits in a cause-effect chain of this complexity. We should encourage the expression of opinions in a pluralistic society because there is no one single causal explanation. These issues have been considered in a publication by the Swedish National Housing Authority (1989) entitled "Environmental and ecological issues in overall planning by municipalities", where one can read (p. 5):

> "Even if many of the connections in the ecosystem are known, each and individually, the relationships between all these connections can work out in completely unknown and unfamiliar ways. Since what can in fact be proved and examined through empirical experiments is only a tiny fraction of the process we take part in and influence, we must accept a great many uncertainties."

The study of cybernetics in this section will try to explain where the uncertainties are, what they consist of and how, through the use of GLST, they can be described and communicated, thus contributing to an increase in our knowledge of our situation. *Figures 9:4, 9:5,* and *9:6* illustrate the complexity of the cybernetic process and the problem of interpreting connections in the feedback process. The decider subsystem is inadequate for the demands placed on it. *Figure 9:4* shows the feedback process at each level cell – the Earth and from the highest level – the Earth to the cell. Only one subsystem, the decider, is shown. The decider subsystem is here assumed to have several echelons and components. The figure shows a feedback process which is assumed to move from one level to the next level up, and shows feedback processes between plant and animal cells and the Earth. Together with the feedback processes between subsystems within each level and feedback processes illustrated in *Figures 9:5,* and *9:6* the degrees of freedom are infinite which may be one of the prerequisites of self-organizing and evolution.

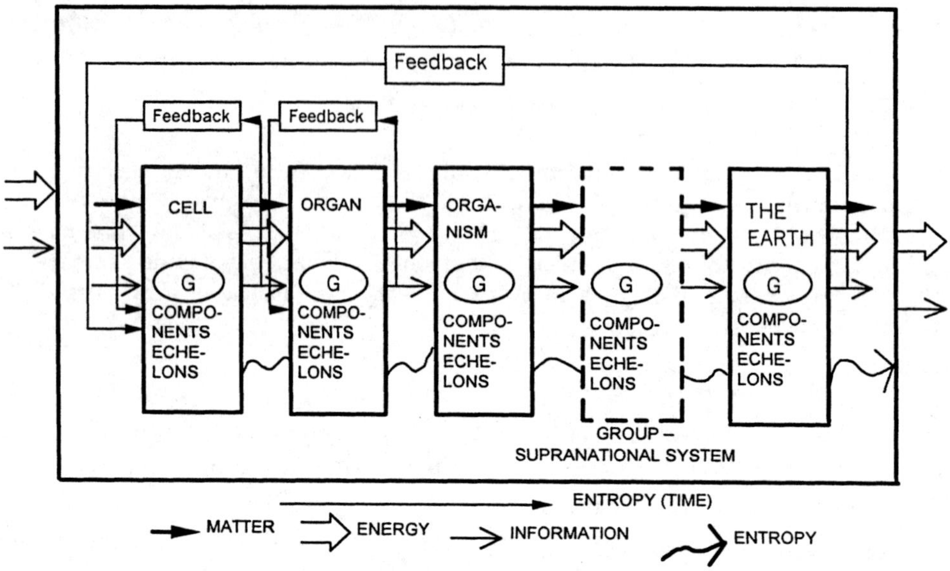

Figure 9:4 Feedback lines from and to: the cell, the organ, organism, group, organization, society, supranational system and the Earth. T. Frandberg 1991.

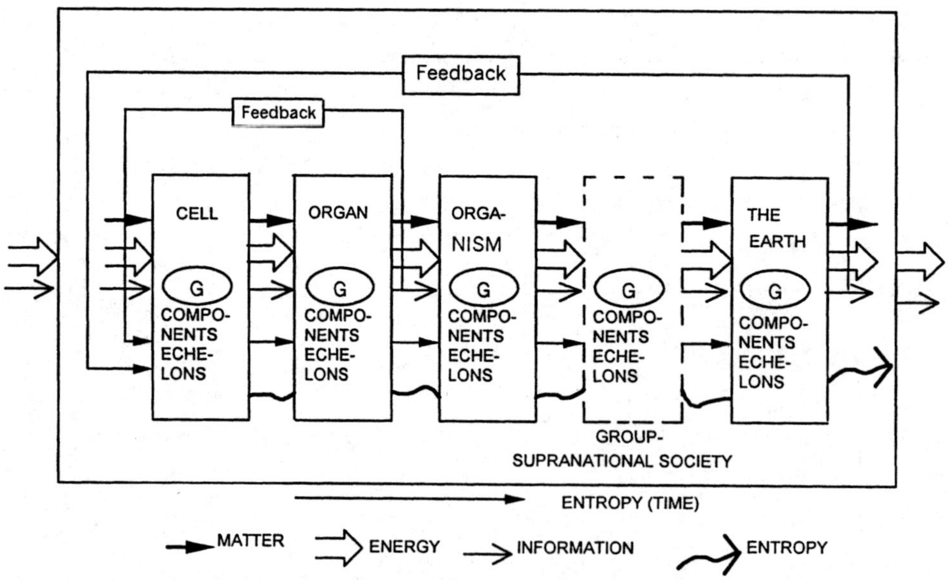

Figure 9:5 shows the feedback processes between one level and the next level above, *e. g. between cell and organ. T. Frandberg 1991.*

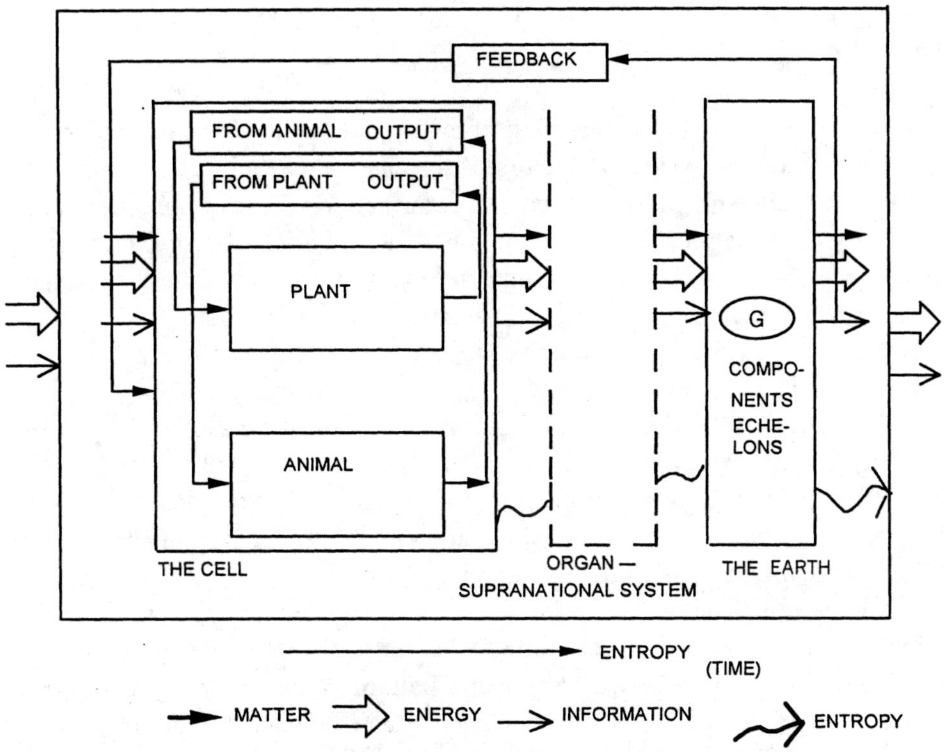

Figure 9:6 Feedback processes between plant and animal cells and between cells and the Earth. T. Frandberg 1991.

Time Aspects

Hawking (1988 p. 153) says: "The increase of disorder or entropy with time is one example of what is called an arrow of time, something that distinguishes the past from the future, given a direction to time." *Figure 1:2* shows living systems going into states of increasing entropy. It is then necessary to study this process in relation to time in order to see if and how this arrow can be reconciled with the thermodynamic arrow of time. When one examines a cybernetic process one is dependent on observing the time interval between an implemented measure and its effect. In living systems there will be different time intervals according to whether one looks at the speed of the impulses in the nerve cells or changes in the parts of the skeleton, as is pointed out in Rose (1988). In connection with the cybernetic process Miller says that the speed with which the signal is transmitted can be of decisive importance.

Figure 5:1 showing a planning process leading to "Rational" planning, takes no account of these vital factors. If the channel capacity is insufficient or if "the free citizen" does not receive information, for example because it comes too late the pluralistic society is not doing its job. The capacity of the whole system for information transmission as it is shown in for example *Figures 9:2* must not be blocked. The problems are increasingly difficult to solve at the level of society and the cybernetic process increasingly difficult to interpret, as is indicated in *Figures 12:6, 9:4, 9:5* and *9:6*.

Transmission via the information and communication system takes place through the study of data bases, communication networks, relational networks and information networks. Samuelson (1978) has given examples of "Network Hybrid", "Relational Network", "Cellular System with Communications", and "Communication across Cellular System".

A change that arises at cell level due to changes at the level of society might not perhaps be understood until the survival of the cell is irrevocably threatened (see *Figure 7:7)*. The opposite state of affairs can also be imagined when a change in a cell, organ or organism can threaten the survival of the system. The time difference existing between different levels must also be taken into account. What is needed is to find some factors of which one can say that they represent the entropy increase, for example, the ozone hole, and then place these in relation to the energy consumption per unit of time. In so doing it will be necessary to summate the consumption of energy at the different levels. At the level of society and the Earth. FRN (1987 Källa 28) refers to two alternative explanations for the changes of the ozone layer. One alternative (The Dynamic Explanation Model) is that the changes mainly depend on changes in the movements in the lower stratosphere mass of air. The second alternative (The Chemical Explanation Model) maintains that the depletion of the ozone layer mainly stems from industrially produced freon. This alternative shows that the changes are dependent on the amount of freon gases used in different industries. By using simulation according to the model suggested here it would be possible to use these figures for further analyses of the effects on for example industrial employment, and subsystems at different levels. One example of reporting on our global consumption of energy is to be found in Behavioral Science vol.24, No.4, May 1974. There are also good yardsticks in Wellburn (1988) and the hierarchical order is also noted there.

Before we proceed to examples of simulation I would like to look at an issue which has to do with values and validity. This issue concerns the question of how, within the framework of Living Systems, the result of a simulation are applied. Another issue which is closely connected with this is how quality of life can be expressed in terms of Living Systems and modelled-based simulations.

Chapter 10

VALUES

It may be inconvenient to take up such a vast field as values in a short chapter like this. It is a subject which ought to be left to another, more wide-ranging discussion. However, my intention here is limited to paying attention to the question of the connection between values and human survival. On (p. 392) it is stated in Bunge (1989) that we all live by our values. If our values are right we may be saved, and we shall succumb if the prevailing value systems are wrong. It is the root of our woes that values and morals have biological and social roots. This is shown in *Figure 10:1* and the following text which is taken from (p. 16).

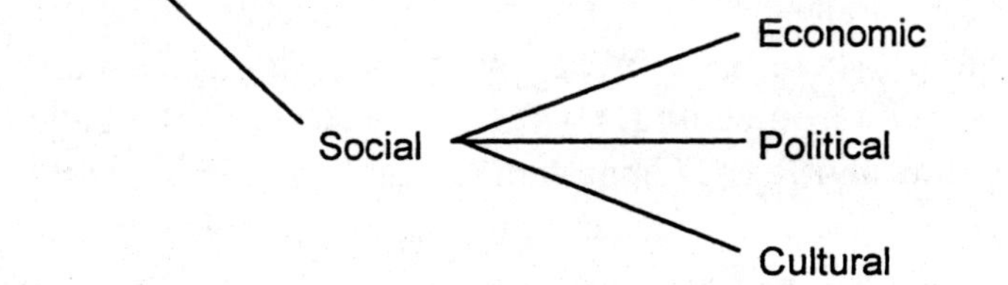

Figure 10:1 Showing values partitioned into two large families biological and social. Source Bunge 1989.

Every genus may be split into cognitive, moral, and aesthetic. Some objects are polyvalent, i.e. they are valuable or disvaluable in more than one respect. For example, a loaf of bread is both biologically and economically valuable. Bunge concludes this chapter entitled "Value Theory" by saying that: "No general value calculus is possible because the value of a whole depends not only on the nature of its components but also of their links, hence on the value of the emergent properties of the whole." The subject of values seems perhaps at first sight not to be connected with living systems. However, at the end of Bunge (1989) (p. 393) it is concluded that the summum bonum of the value system which has been advocated in his book is human survival. Moreover, human beings must be able at least to imagine what good life is like, if they are to bother doing something to save humankind. Bunge has a supreme norm: "Enjoy life and help live".

Howard Odum has opened a discussion on the connection between values, morals, ethics, and energy and says in Odum (1976) (p. 11) that basic laws of energy apparently apply to all human processes and all processes of nature, including economics, culture, and aesthetics. Lowrence (1985 p. 255) wonders if individual scientists are not mostly guided by personal motives and morals rather than grand ethical schemes. It can therefore be difficult to see how individual scientists' actions can be oriented to "society's values". This touches on the question asked in Bunge (1989) where it is said that when we abstract values from their bearers we make the same mistake as when we detach properties from the things possessing them. Are the values of society, or can become, always the same as the values of individual subjects, and how can the interaction between values of society and values of subjects be interpreted and understood? "Ethics and science are related in two ways: there is the ethics of science research and there is the science of ethics, or scientific ethics. The former is the investigation of the moral code governing scientific research, whereas the science of ethics is the scientific study of the roots and function of moral codes". How should scientific research freedom be balanced against societal? There is a need for a long term scanning of global environmental and resource issues, with a view toward anticipating problems, identifying policy and R & D opportunities, and stimulating responses. There is, with varying degrees of emphasis, a focus on dialogue and action. It may be impossible to say how the interaction of values of society and subjects has developed up till now.

According to Bunge (1989) science is not alien to values. First because the scientific investigator holds certain psychological values such as curiosity, ingenuity and honesty; semantic values such as clear meaning and maximal truth; and methodological values such as testability and precision. Second, because developmental and social psychologists, as well as anthropologists, sociologists, and political scientists, are supposed to study value systems in a scientific manner. Third, because social scientists, particularly those of the applied kind, cannot help making value judgements, such as poverty is degrading and greed breeds violence. At the level of society with regard to the process of the subsystem decider Miller refers to A. Etzioni where he states (p. 804) that values are not given. They are fluid and affected by the decisions as well as affecting them. Values and facts, means and ends cannot be separated by decision-makers.

VALIDITY

There is a need to discuss the relation between value and validity. We can define validity as an expression of how a statement or the result of an action expresses what its value originally was related to. According to Samuelson (1978 b p. 82) "the fact that validity actually measures (and is influenced by) factors other than we want to measure lowers its validity." Validity is related to what we want, and accordingly to values. An action may for example have a result which is related to a value which perhaps might have changed over a period of time. It is also necessary to discuss how and when values are changed. Miller (1978) puts forward five types of validity (p. 85):

- Internal validity or reliability (as when repeated simulations give the expected result regardless of the internal relations in the model)
- Face validity (the impression of realism the simulation gives to the experimenter or participant)
- Variable-parameter validity (when through repeated simulations with small systematic changes one observes results)
- Event validity (when one, over time, compares the results of the simulation with what really emerges)
- Hypothesis validity (specific limited hypotheses can produce high validity while general hypotheses with low validity may be more

valuable scientifically since they relate to a greater number of different systems).

In this section, my use of the term 'validity' is closest to face validity and hypothesis validity. When the question of validity is linked with the problem of acquiring data one sees the difficulty of reaching what in these respects is the more limited validity represented by the definitions of internal validity, variable-parameter validity and event validity. The question of validity is also linked to the question of reliability, which here corresponds most closely to variable-parameter validity. It can in addirion be linked with predictability, which corresponds most closely to event validity. Advocates, although they represent the same subject area, have valuations which mean that even when using the same data they can come to divergent results. The above is close to what Steinar Kvale writes and develops in Kvale (1987) under the heading "To validate Is to Investigate" (p. 77): "Validation becomes investigation, continually checking, questioning, and theoretically interpreting the finding." When the question of validity and reliability is taken up it often meets with the comment that it is close to a positivistic approach as in Bailey (1990). In Kvale (1989) the discussion on quantitative and qualitative measures resembles that which takes place with regard to the differences between hard and soft systems.

Chapter 11

QUALITY OF LIFE

Peter Caws conducts in Caws (1989) a historical review of the emergence of political economy. He makes an interesting comparison, comparable with Johannisson (1988), between the emergence of political economy and the emergence of numbers. He writes that the concepts seem from the beginning to have come about in connection with the acquisition and distribution of goods (numerous is connected with the Greek nemo, to deal out, dispense). Davies (1992) also sees (p. 108) the beginning of simple arithmetic with very mundane practical matters, from which point then mathematics took on a life and existence of its own. Caws says that quantitative and qualitative do not divide up a territory, they both cover it, overlapping almost totally. But one is basic and the other is optional. Everything in our world is qualitative; and everything is capable — given suitable ingenuity on our part — of generating quantitative determinations. In Rosen (1991 p. 3) starting from a quotation from Ernest Rutherford "Qualitative is nothing but poor quantitative" and a quotation from Robert Hutchins "A social scientist is a person who counts telephone pools", there is a characterization of a duality between hard and soft science based on the duality between quantitative and qualitative aspects. Hard science demands that inexact talk about quality is replaced by precise numbers. In soft science the qualities of social structure which are unquantifiable are the most important. One example of how this duality is dealt with is given by the United Bureau of the Census USA, whose main business might seem to be quantitative. The Bureau has nevertheless an interest in questions of the quality of life, and has devoted a good deal of attention to efforts that have been made to translate expressions of satisfaction or dissatisfaction into numerical measures. The standard trick is to develop an ordinal ranking and then assign cardinal values to the positions within it for the purpose of drawing graphs, performing statistical computations, etc. The SIWB (the initials stand for Social Indicators of Well-Being) scale, for example, assigns the integers 1 through 7 to 'terrible', 'unhappy', 'mostly dissatisfied', 'mixed', 'mostly satisfied', 'mostly pleased', and 'delighted'.

One possible use of the results of inquiries on such bases (or improved ones — the Census people seem realistically aware of the shortcomings in the state of the art) might be to produce correlations between those measures and quantities that permit an objective assessment, such as income, energy consumption, cubic feet of living space, number and horsepower of automobiles, etc. as Boulding (1971) discusses in "What do Economic Indicators Indicate? (Quality and Quantity in the GNP) He sees (p. 74) model building as a significant aidmaking fostering make predictions and to the growth of knowledge. But when we get to complex systems — especially macrosystems — there may be a wide gap between statistical significance and epistemological significance. He also sees the danger when radical critics in their love of mankind despise the taste of what he calls a vulgar majority wishing to impose their own more refined taste.

Chapter 12

APPLICATION AND SIMULATION

INTRODUCTION

The choice of simulation as one of the ways to test/understand a theory is supported by Bunge (1973 p. 107) when he says that the possibilities of testability depend on three conditions:

- the possibilities of testability are inversely related to the logical
- strength of the theory
- the possibilities of attaching a model object to a generic theory
- that the general theory or the model (or both) and the data themselves are blameless

Starting from these conditions Bunge continues (p. 118) that concrete simulation behavior may help us to understand the original — which corresponds to our aim here, i.e. communicating and analysing the conditions of the survival of living systems. The above conditions are discussed in the previous chapters.

To begin with we can consider the matrix *Figure 12:1* which shows the 20 critical subsystems

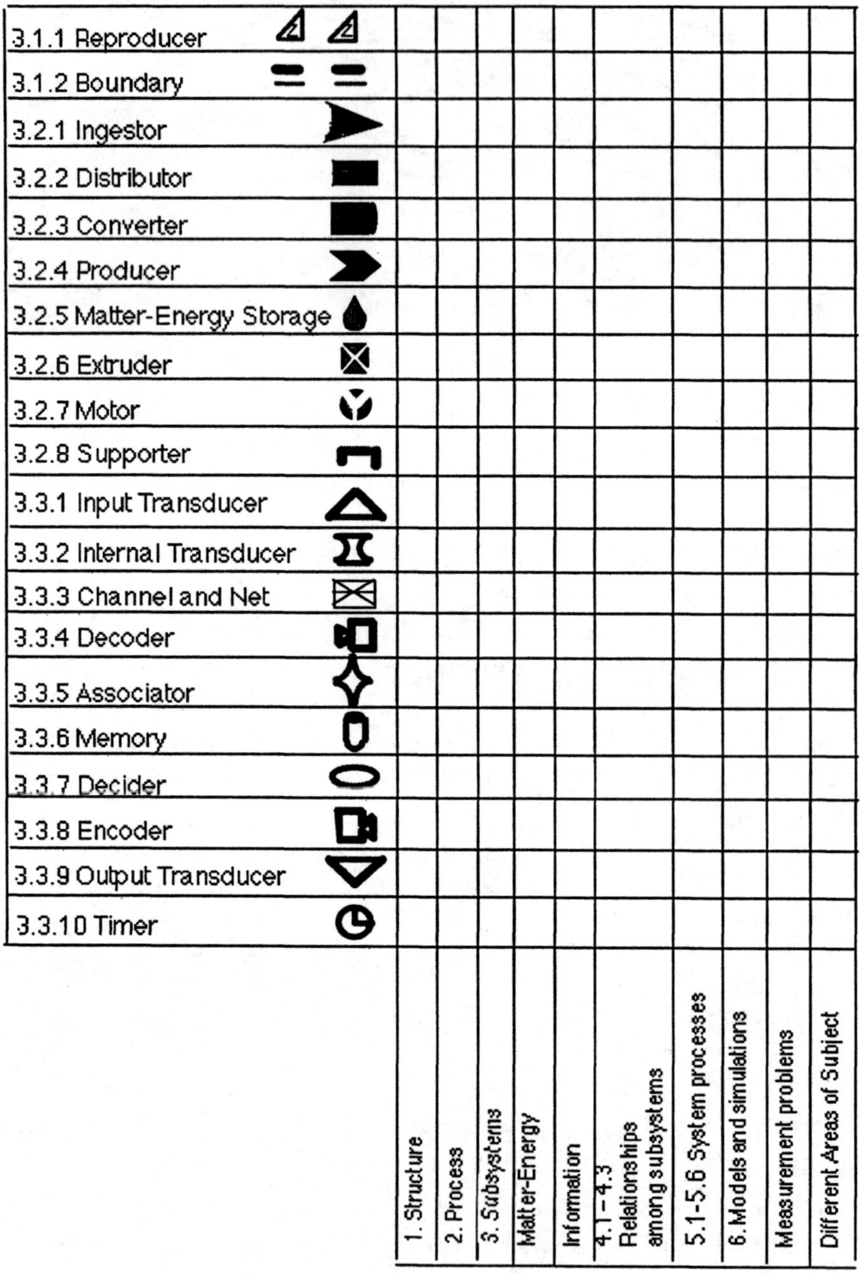

Figure 12:1 The rows show the subsystems with their codes and symbols.

The codes are those indicated in Living Systems and the symbols have been obtained from "The Nature of Living Systems" (p. 157) in Behavioral Science (1990). The columns show in which respect they are studied. *Figure 12:1* is based on "Outline of Chapters 3,4, and 6 through 12" (Miller 1978 pp. xxi-xli) and is the same for the eight levels-(cell, organ, organism, group, organization, community, society, supranational system, and is also here assumed to be valid for the level of the Earth). A column has been added, "Measurement problems" because the problems of acquiring and retrieving data have proved to be an essential aspect in the quantification of the model. A column "Different areas of subject" has also been added to point to the interactive study of the subsystems.

The next figure, *Figure 12:2,* is a basic figure referring to each system's level (cell – the Earth)

The subsystems are quantified according to subsystems in the figure. Changes are over time and how these interact within a systems level and also between subsystems at other levels. The intention is to find measures/quantities which are decisive for the boundaries which determine the survival of the whole system. This is however bound to be a difficult task, as is shown for example in *Figure 7:7* with the sigmoid curvature. At higher levels (especially), there is an absence of data which indicate boundaries for a living system which is self-regulating and self-organizing within the conditions that apply in respect of survival. There has to be enough food and water so the inhabitants can survive. There are examples where communities no longer exist because of the fact that they have been abandoned owing to pollution or floods. These floods may have been caused by impoverishing the soil and this can have relations to subsystems at other levels.

THE CELL, THE TOWN AND THE EARTH

The following *Figures 12:3, 12:4,* and *12:5* which are taken from (Frandberg 1994) contain an overview of the quantified subsystems in STELLA. Initially the quantification was performed for the variables of the community. The variables concerning the level of Earth are not quantified to the same extent. Variables concerning the cell have not been quantified, although subsystems are stated.

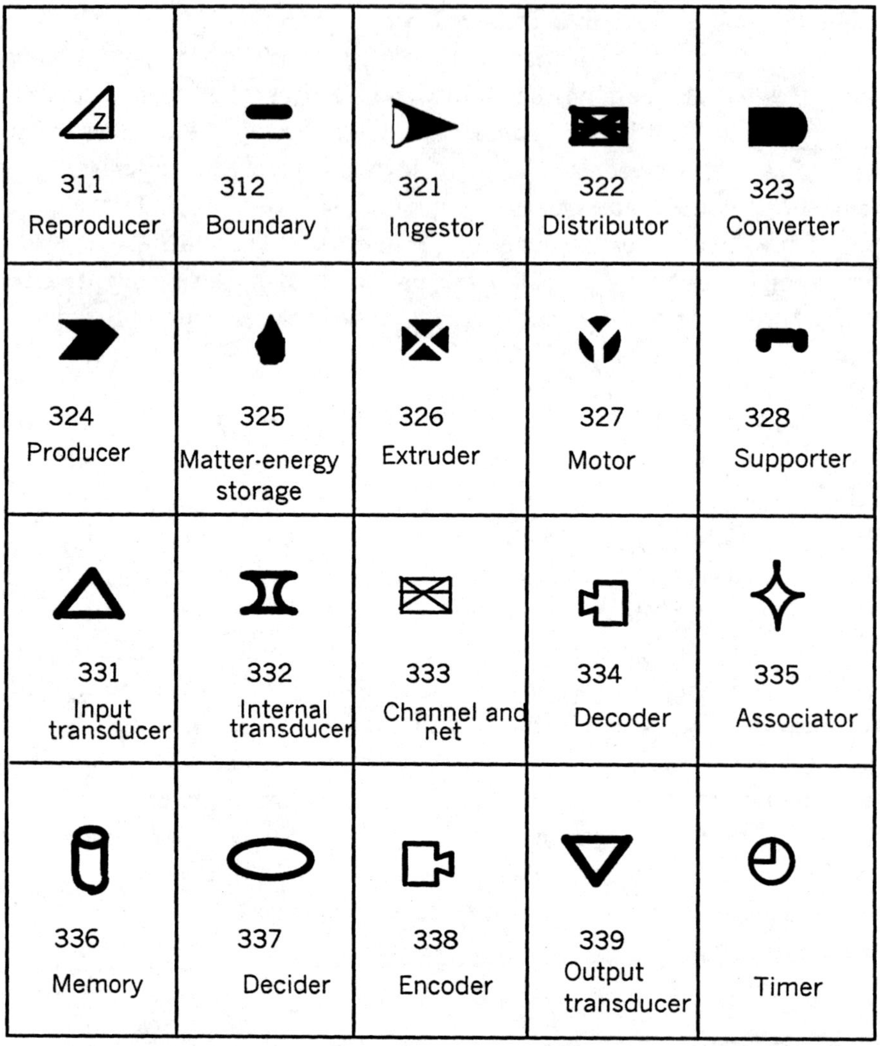

Figure 12:2 Basic figure showing the twenty critical subsystems at each of the nine levels the cell — the Earth.

Chromosomes and cromatin nucleus 311-11 Reproducer	311-12 Reproducer	For matter energy cell membrane plus cell 312-11 Boundary	Cellmembrane as awhole or specialized regions 321-11 Ingestor	Endoplasmic reticulum 322-11 Distributor	Enzymes such as those in mitochondrion 323-11 Converter	Chlorophyll chloroplast enzymes golgi apparatus 324-11 Producer
324-12 Producer	324-13 Producer	324-14 Producer	324-15 Producer	Phosphorylated organic com-pounds glycogen granules 325-11 Matter-energy storage	Region of cell membrane capable of matter-enrgy out of cell 326-11 Extruder	326-12 Extruder
326-13 Extruder	326 -14 Extruder	Cytoplasm Myofibrils 327-11 Motor	328-11 Supporter	Microtubules 328-12 Supporter	Cell wall of plant cells 328-13 Supporter	328-14 Supporter
Cell membrane 328-15 Supporter	QoL Quality of life	Cellmembrane particularly sites specialzed of cell receptor 331-11 Input transducer	Enzymer and repressor molecules 332-11 Internal transducer	332-12 Internal transducer	Endoplasmic reticulum 333-11 Channel and net	Molecule binfing sites 334-11 Decoder
Unknown 335-11 Associator	Unknown 336-11 Memory	Regulator genes and operon 337-11 Decider	Components producing alpha-coded antibenic proteins 338-11 Encoder	Cellmembrane presynaptic membrane 339-11 Output transducer	Timer	

Figure 12:3 shows an example of subsystems at the level of cell

The rectangle/page QoL leaves room for an attribute or a kind of index which can be used in order to compare results when alternative simulations are made.

Dwellings housholds Dwellings by type 311--61 Reproducer	Population by by sex and age 311-62 Reproducer	Harbour Airport Railway staion 312-61 Boundary	Harbour Airport Railway-station 321-61 Ingestor	Traffic Roads Bridges Tunnels 322-61 Distributor	Consumption of energy type of use and raw material 323-61 Converter	Production volume 324-61 Producer
Gainfully emplyoed pop. from age 16 324-62 Producer	Employd industrial persons by occupation 324-63 Producer	New consruction 324-64 Producer	Newconstruc-tion of nonresidential floor space 324-65 Producer	Consumption of energy Different fields 325-61 Matter-energy storage	Pollution from sewage 326-61 Extruder	Pollution from from garbage 326-62 Extruder
Air pollution from energy production 326-63 Extruder	Air pollution from traffic 326-64 Extruder	SL Greater Stockholm SJ Swedish Railways Trucks Cars 327-61 Motor	Dwellings in houses by size multi-family 328-61 Supporter	Public medical health 328-62 Supporter	Dwellings in small houses by size 328-63 Supporter	Hospitals BedsHospital treatment 326-64 Supporter
Social services 328-64 Supporter	QoL 331-6 Quality of life	Administrative units of the City Input transducer	Mailing servic Press 332-61 Internal transducer	TV Administrative Departments 332-62 Internal transducer	Tele and other communication facilities 333-6 Channel and net	Administrative units of the city 334-6 Decoder
Municipal employees by employment 335-6 Associator	Databases and other forms of documentatio 336-6 Memory	The city council 337-6 Decider	Administrative departments information centre 338-6 Encoder	TV Radio Administrate departments Mailing 339-6 Output transducer	Timer	

Figure 12:4 Overview of subsystems and components at the level of community

Plants and animals.Chemi-cal and physical processes 311-91 Reproducer	311-91 Reproducer	Atmosphere 312-91 Boundary	Atmosphere 321-91 Ingestor	Water and air 322-91 Distributor	Organizations which convert matter and energy 323-91 Converter	Plant and animal resources 324-91 Producer
324-92 Producer	Industrial production 324-93 Producer	Agriculture production 324-94 Producer	Energy production 324-95 Producer	Natural and recources 325-91 Matter-energy storage	326-91 Extruder	326-92 Extruder
Atmosphere 326-93 Extruder	Extruder for matter is lacking 326.94 Extruder	327-91 Motor	Land 328-91 Supporter	Water 328-92 Supporter	Air 328-93 Supporter	328-94 Supporter
328-95 Supporter	QoL Quality of life	Registration of energy flows 331-91 Input transducer	UN subsystems 332-91 Internal transducer	332-92 Internal transducer	Satellites and other forms of communication 333-91 Channel and net	UN subsystems 334-91 Decoder
UN Subsystems 335-91 Associator	UN's statistical and other reports 336-91 Memory	UN 337-91 Decider	UN subsystems 338-91 Encoder	UN subsystems 339-91 Output transducer	Timer	

Figure 12:5 Overview of subsystems and components at the level of Earth.

Cross-Level Analysis of Extruder

Cross-level analyses of Extruder at the levels of the cell, the community and the Earth are assumed to be effected according to *Figure 12:6*.

The left-hand portion describes the connection between extruder (L326-11, L326-61 and L326-91 described in *Figures 12:8, 12:9* and *12:10* at the levels of the cell, the community and the Earth. This connection is not seen separately from the connections within each system level. As the extruder is also determined through the conditions for interaction of the 20 critical subsystems, a feedback process that takes place between and within levels can also be taken into account.

The state of affairs in connection with *Figures 9:4, 9:5*, and *9:6* below shows that there remains the question of ascertaining the total quantity of input and output represented by each level. If one held a deterministic view of society it is likely that one would shrink from trying to describe reality. It seems far too complex, and so one might adopt a philosophical approach and say that the description cannot be discussed using a theory as a basis.

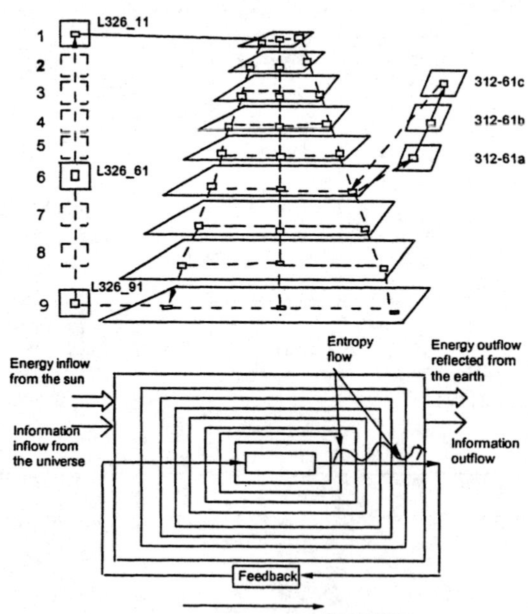

Figure 12:6 shows the nine levels with feedback lines.

The subsystem extruder is studied at the levels of cell, community and the Earth. The subsystem extruder is also studied as consisting of subsubsystems. In cells of a certain type, and as a part of the cell membrane, extruder exhibits a degree of complexity which in Herrman (1989) that takes nine chapters to explain, accompanied by a great many references. The description shows that we still cannot decide what the connection between and within the cell's extruder and the other subsystems of the cell really looks like. The difference between input and output requires further explanation.

How far are we to go in mapping connections in order to obtain a basis for a decision? We are obliged to strike a balance concerning the usefulness of complexity in a model. see *Figure 7:6*. A cross-level analysis shows the defects that exist when we wish to observe the connections between different levels. When metabolic waste is emitted at the level of community it is possible to show how the emissions interfere with the cell and the Earth over time. An arrow of time has been entered under the entropy arrow in *Figure 12:11*.

The next question is: How can the rate of increase be changed?

In fact developments are moving towards increasing use of energy as a result of man's intervention, which here is assumed can lead to increasing entropy. At the level of community Extruder can be defined as the management of garbage tips, sewage treatment works, exhaust systems on road vehicles, smoke from chimneys (downward dispersed), incinerators etc. Output from Extruder at the level of the community must in its turn be handled by Extruder at the level of society and then the supranational system, and will in the end be a burden on the Earth. At the level of Earth there is no subsystem Extruder that can transfer to the Universe that output which emanates from the input of matter to the lower levels. The consequence is that all activities that cannot be subjected to these conditions must be reduced, and this calls into question the social system that now prevails in the industrialized part of the world. In Luft '90 (Air '90) there are several examples which indicate that we are running out of time. It is estimated that the global effects of different emissions could result in an increase in temperature throughout the world if the present development is allowed to continue unchanged.

There does however exist disagreement on these issues between different researchers. Nierenberg, and Seitz (1990) have questioned the reliability of the Greenhouse predictions. They have in a Figure 1 (p. 9) shown the predictions of the rise in sea level resulting from the greenhouse effect, plotted against the year in which the prediction was made. The predictions decreased from 25 feet in 1980 to three feet in 1985 and to one foot in 1989.

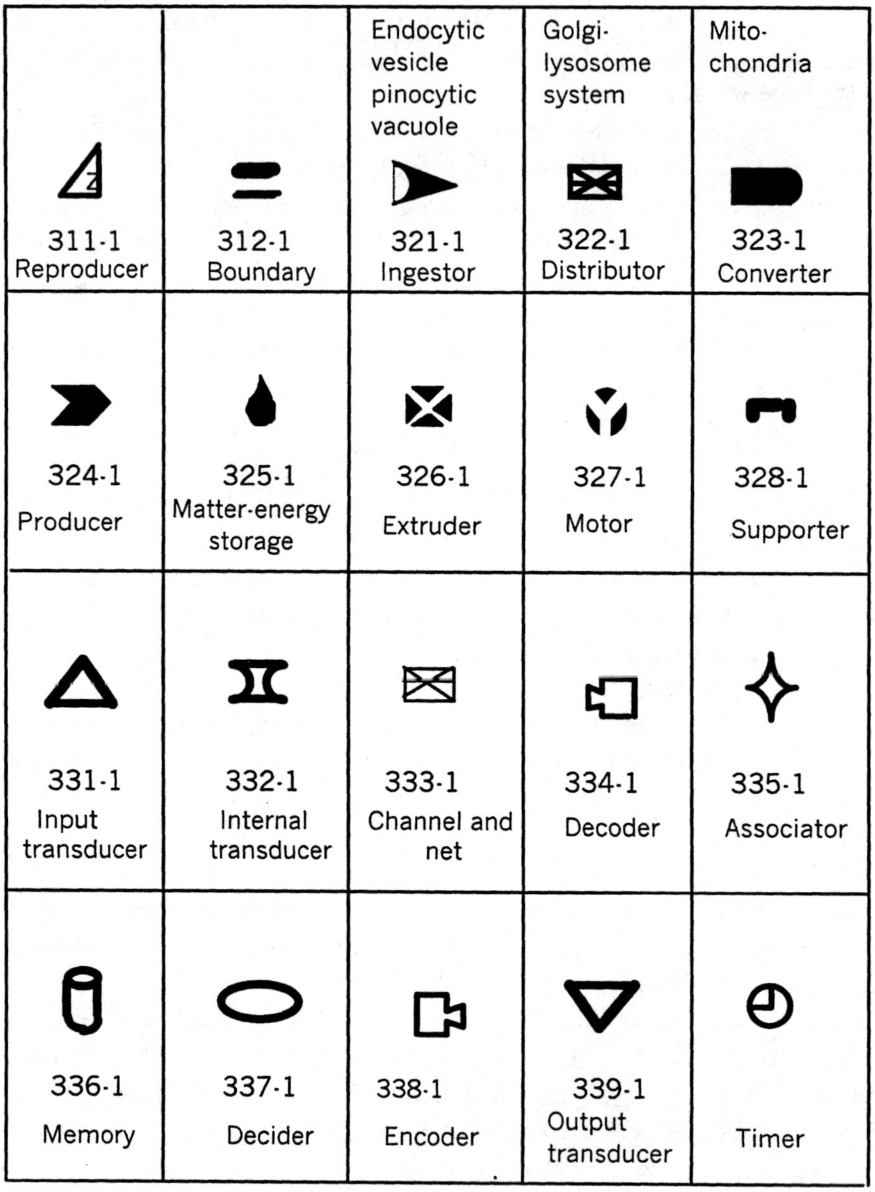

Figure 12:8 Extruder at the level of cell.

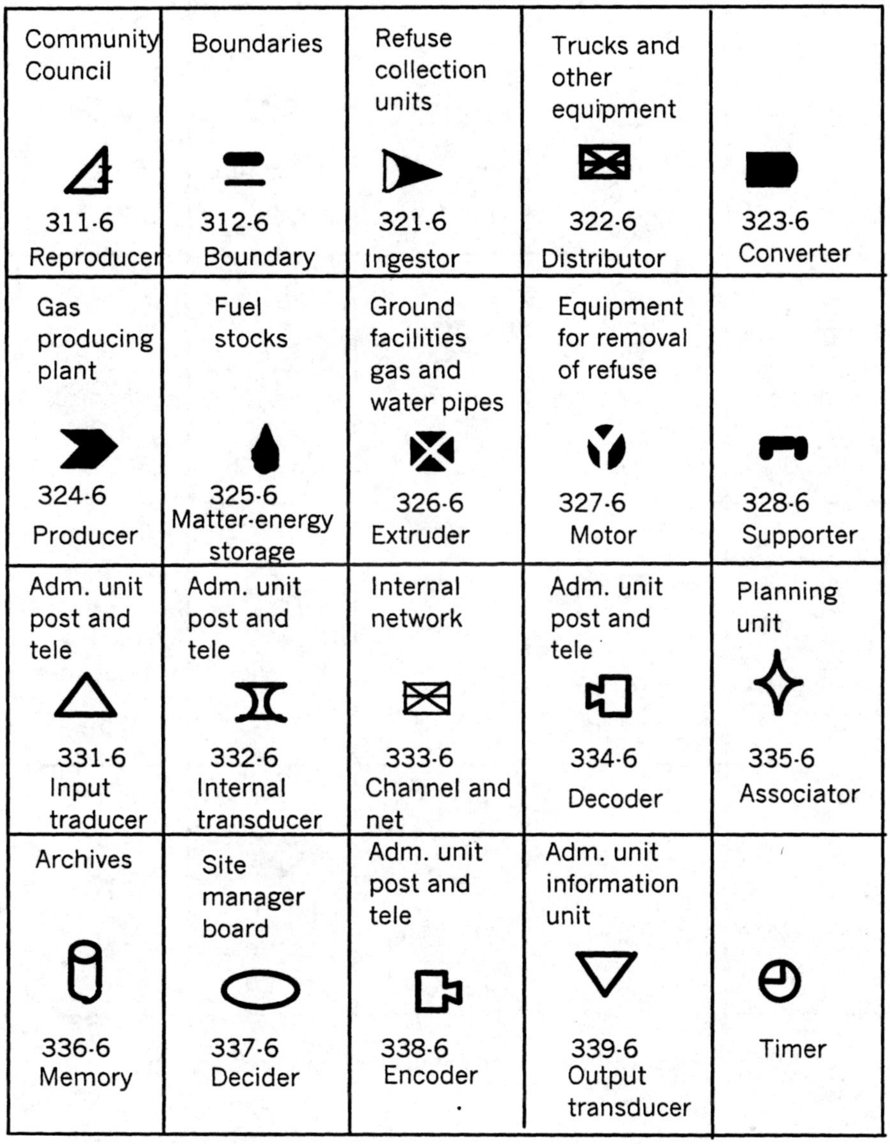

Figure 12:9 Extruder at the level of community

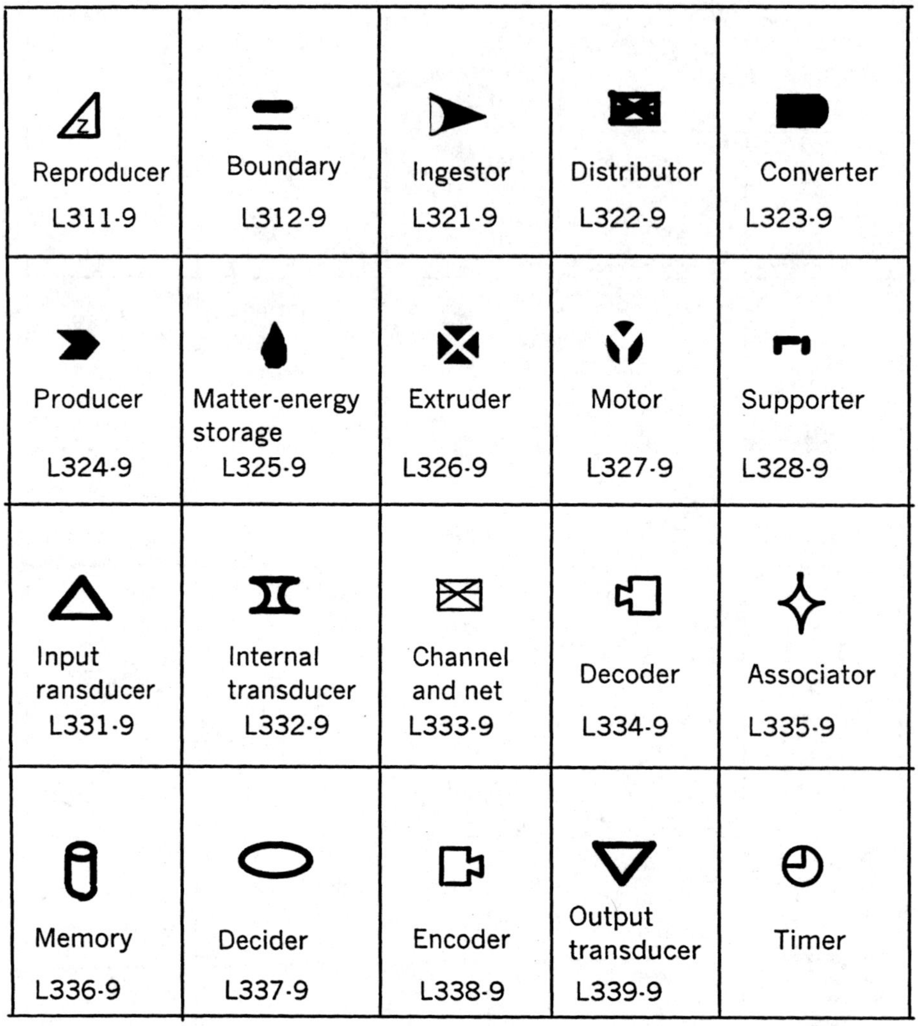

Figure 12:10 Extruder at the level of the Earth.

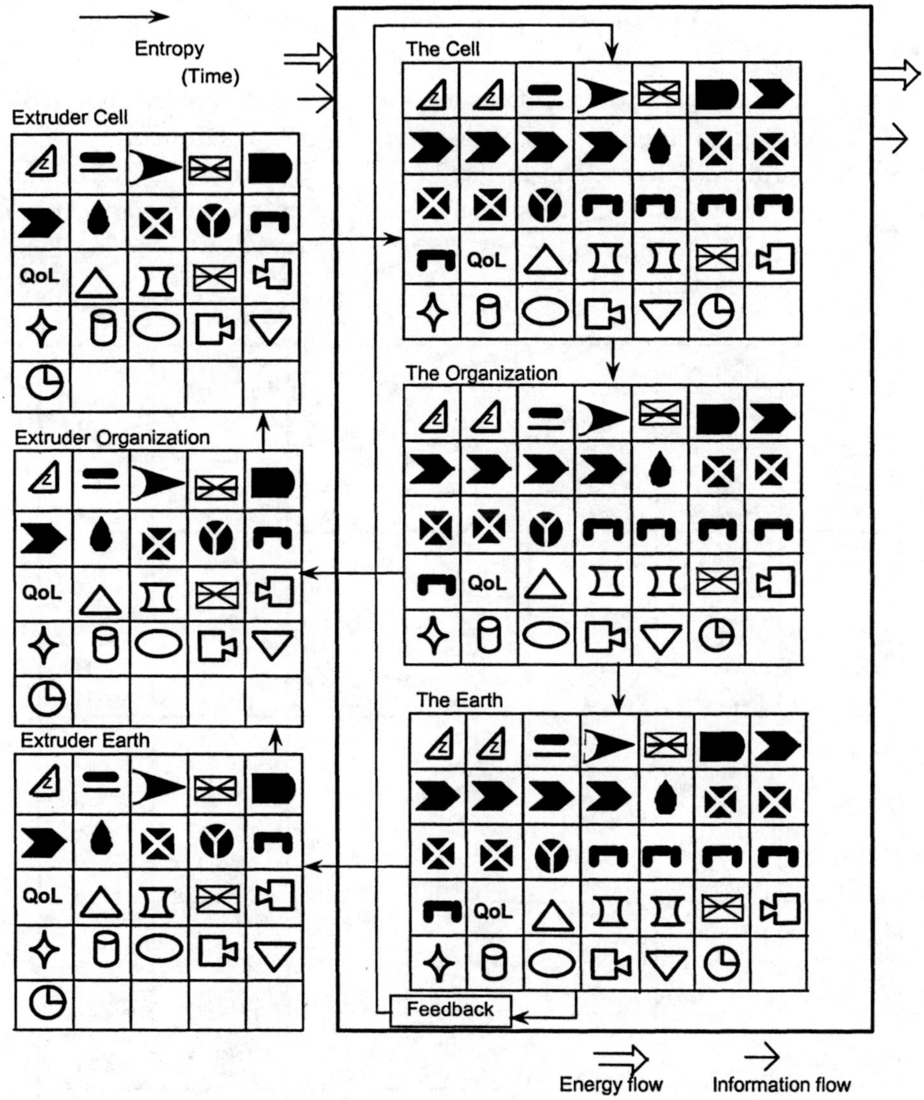

Figure 12:11 shows a compilation of Figures 12:8, 12:9, 12:10 (extruder at different levels) and Figures 12:3 cell, 12:4 community and 12:5 the Earth, showing interactions between systems, subsystems and components. Lines with small arrows symbolize feedback. T. Frandberg 1991.

DIFFERENT LEVELS OF BOUNDARY

As is the case with extruder, the subsystem boundary can be analysed at levels according to *Figure 12:11* and *Figure 12:7* with retention of the connection to the whole system. In the same way *Figures 12:12, 12:13,* and *12:14* which are taken from (Frandberg 1994) show the boundary 312-5a, 312-5b, and 312-5c at different levels. *Figure 30* shows how these levels can be related to the system.

311-6al Reproducer	Railway station 312-6al Boundary	Airport 3.12-6a2 Boundary	Harbour 312-6a3 Boundary	Truck terminal 312-6a4 Boundary	Bus terminal 312-6a5 Boundary	Water works 321-6al Ingestor
Custom station 321-6a2 Ingestor	Railway track Road 322-6al Distributor	Transformer station 323-6al Converter	Hotel 324-6al Producer	Oil refinery 325-6al Matter-energy storage	Sewage treatment works 326-6al Extruder	Waste dumping 326-6a2 Extruder
326-6a3 Extruder	326-6a4 Extruder	Defences 327-61a Motor	Buildings 328-61a Supporter	Road 328-6a2 Supporter	Bridge 328-6a3 Supporter	328-6a4 Supporter
328-6a5 Supporter	QoL Quality of life	Different kinds of ekectronic terminals 331-6al Input transducer	Supervision traffic signals 332-6al Internal transducer	332-6a2 Internal transducer	Communication networks of different kinds 333-6al Channel and net	Immigration office 334-6al Decoder
Planning department of the city 335-6al Associator	Databases and statistic reports 336-6al Memory	Councilor 337-6al Decider	Tourist information and tcentre of information 338-6al Encoder	Post terminals Differentkinds electronic terminals 339-6al Output transducer	Timer	

Figure 12:12 Subsystem (312-5a) and components of the subsystem boundary at the level of community See Figure 30

Local community authority 311-6b1 Reproducer	Border of different administrative units 312-6b1 Boundary	Shore 31.2-6b2 Boundary	Administrativ departments for equipment of different kinds 321-6b1 Ingestor	Railway tracks, roads 322-6b2 Distributor	Oil refinery Transformer stations 323-6b1 Converter	Harbour cranes 324-6b1 Producer
Employes workers 324-6b2 Producer	Employes administrative 324-6b3 Producer	324-6b4 Producer	324-6b5 Producer	Oilcisterns 325-6b1 Matter-energy storage	Harbour cranes 326-6b1 Extruder	Police 326-6b2 Extruder
Packing department 326-6b3 Extruder	326-6b4 Extruder	Maintenance personal of machine systems 327-6b1 Motor	Harbour buildings 328-6b1 Supporter	Office buildings 328-6b2 Supporter	Quays 328-6b3 Supporter	328-6b4 Supporter
328-6b5 Supporter	QoL Quality of life	Electronic equipment information centre 331-6b1 Input transducer	332-6b1 Internal transducer	Department responsible for informatio 332-6b2 Internal transducer	Communi-cation networks 333-6b1 Channel and net	Administrative departments for ships arrivals departures 334-6b1 Decoder
Harbour authorities Planning departments 335-6b1 Associator	Databases 336-6b1 Memory	Councillor 337-6b1 Decider	List of rates 338-6b1 Encoder	Electronic equipment information centre 339-6b1 Output transducer	Timer	

Figure 12:13 Subsystem (312-5b) and components of the subsystem boundary at the level of community. See Figure 30

The local community authority 311-6c1 Reproducer	Border of different administra tive units 312-6c1 Boundary	312-6c2 Boundary	Administra-tive depart-ments 321-6c1 Ingestor	Railway tracks roads 322-6c1 Distributor	Oil refinary Transformer stations 323-6c1 Converter	324-6c1 Producer
Employees Workers 324-6c2 Producer	Employees Administra-tive 324-6c3 Producer	324-6c4 Producer	324-6c5 Producer	Supply depots 325-6c6 Matter-energy storage	Drainage 326-6c1 Extruder	326-6c2 Extruder
326-6c1 Extruder	326-6c2 Extruder	Maintenance personal 327-6c1 Motor	328-6c1 Supporter	328-6c2 Supporter	328-6c3 Supporter	328-6c4 Supporter
328-6c5 Supporter	QoL Quality of life	Electronic equipment 331-6c1 Input transducer	332-6c1 Internal transducer	Manager responsible for information 332-6c2 Internal transducer	Communi-cation networks 333-6c1 Channel and net	Administra-tive departments 334-6c1 Decoder
Planning depart-ments 335-6c1 Associator	Maps blueprints 336-6c1 Memory	Manager 337-6c1 Decider	Code communi-cations 338-6c1 Encoder	Electronic equipment 339-6c1 Output transducer	Timer	

Figure 12:14 Subsystem (312-5c) and components of the subsystem boundary at the level of community See Figure 12:7

It is not assumed that all interactions between system levels have to be studied as taking place via the boundary at the level of the system, nor that matter-energy and information flows pass through the critical subsystems in a certain order at each system level. Subsystems at different levels such as the cell, the community and the Earth should be seen as directly interacting with each other see *Figure 12:7* with connections showing vertical as well as horizontal links. Otherwise the implication would be that, for example, a boundary and an ingestor could be burdened with the task of distributing and handling all matter-energy and information flows from each and every one of the subsystems to and from the system level. That which is produced through the producer at community level, for example pollutants, will, via the extruder, interact directly with a producer or another critical subsystem at the level of the cell and/or the level of the Earth.

Chapter 12 points to the connections between the cell and the Earth, viewing them as elements of an hierarchy. The comprehensive *Figure 1:1* shows a resemblance to the viewpoint set out in GLST and shows interaction between the Earth, the organism, the organ, and the cell with regard to the compounds that are formed when sulphur (S) joins with oxygen (O2) and (N2) and affects cell, organ and organism. At the level of the cell are noted several critical subsystems, how they are affected within the cell and how the cell is related to the organ and the organism. Wellburn provides a basis for quantifying the effect to which the structure and processes of the cell are subjected in their interaction between the levels of the community and the Earth. The model is constructed along similar lines to Living Systems, though with the difference that information processing subsystems are not accounted for.

Wellburn's model is of one of the studies which have been carried out with the aim of quantifying and understanding how dangerous substances affect the environment. It is valuable because it sees quantification of the interaction between different levels as enriching the simulation of living systems. In the first five chapters of Wellburn (1988) there are descriptions of how sulphur dioxide, nitrogen-based air pollutants, acid rain, ozone, PAN and photochemical smog and other pollutants - global as well as local - come into existence and affect the environment. In a sixth chapter there is a discussion of "Interactions, recent forest decline" and other considerations.

DATA COLLECTION AND STATISTICS

A quotation from Warfield (1976 p. 128) points out that the result of for example a simulation perhaps mostly will depend on the way in which data are processed:

> "While it is often said that one of the main problems in planning is to acquire data, it is possible to observe competing organizations which appear to have access to the same data, but generate radically different results. This suggests that the role of data in planning, while important, is probably less important than the way they are used - that is the preparation of the mind of the manager to interpret and use the data in seeking to realize desired events."

In this light, an important factor is to show the sources of the data (this is of course valid for all presentation of simulation and other reports) but this may be more important when it comes to showing data from such a vast area as represented by living Systems when the task is to interpret results of a simulation and compare them with alternatives, then in order to allow a critical scrutiny it is of decisive importance that data which are used are easily available. The Internet provides many possibilities to find data but one drawback is the large amount of information. The richness of details is overwhelming and it can be difficult to acquire an overview. Systems thinking can then be a means to structure and collect information.

CONTROL PROBLEMS

The boundary has been depicted by the critical subsystems in *Figures 12:12, 12:13* and *12:14*. The danger involved in this way of describing reality is that one could find oneself in a situation which resembles a situation where calculations are made with a limited purpose in view and from a limited perspective regarding what quantity of all products and services is to be produced, how these are to be transported and how the products are to be produced and distributed. My aim here is to ascertain what it is that enables a living system to survive and ensure that interests and constituents of the society have access to the information they feel they need, at the right time and at little cost. This meets the objection that systems science has a normative effect that is not taken into account. We may never be able to demonstrate the influence of normative effects on our decisions but there is an increased possibility that the influence they have will be openly accounted for. There are those who maintain that if people merely give expression to their subjectivity by means of critical heuristic reasoning, then through the democratic process society will progress. However, the drawback is — on what are they to base their subjective understanding? There must/ought to be some form of basic link with reality that can be described and discussed between different subject groups and interests. The implication of a given model must be made clear — a point which is discussed previously in Chapter 5.

Forrester (1988) (p. 47) presents in "Lessons from System Dynamics Modelling" viewpoints which are also emphasized when simulating living systems. A system dynamics model can be created on a desktop computer, which facilitates conversation. Software advances, especially STELLA, facilitate the interaction between mental models and computer models. However, in Forrester (1988) Alexander N. Christakis (p. 38) expresses the view that

> "the rationalistic tradition, inherited from Newtonian mechanics, has been an impediment to the development of a relevant social science paradigm. The preoccupation with pseudo-rigor (e.g. Urban Dynamics or the Club of Rome World Dynamics Project) has been practised at the expense of relevance."

He adds that science must be described as a co-operative social venture and that social science must build on this by recognizing the significance of explicating and interpreting the diversity of perceptions and meanings among the various social groups. Basically one can agree with this statement but one objection that can be made to Christakis is that he himself is pursuing a hazardous path when he speaks of "perceptions and meanings of various social groups." When society is divided into social groups by some form of classification one is at once faced with the problem of how to demarcate different "social groups", how social groups are to be described and how they interact. There may be different values/opinions within a social group so that it cannot always be defined as a homogenous entity. Carlsson (1968) writes about social stratification and mobility and presents as examples seven stratification variables which can underlie a system of division into classes or strata. These are:

a) role played in the productive economy (employer or employee)
b) financial resources (consumption role)
c) prestige, social standing
d) power or influence
e) ideology, political goals, perceived social interest
f) upbringing, cultural attributes, “life style”
g) social intercommunication, contact system.

Additional points can be made concerning human behavior and the processes behind the flow of actions in the social system. How are we to characterise meanings and perceptions belonging to different groups when they are so difficult to describe and when it is even more difficult to indicate how the groups are to be linked to the significance and explications of other groups. The development of society is in many cases steered by interests which on many issues cut right across party and group programs. The question of the environment, for example, is one such issue on which people belonging to established parties can have divergent views or views which lie near other parties/groups. By avoiding the problem of linking proposals for measures, for example as regards energy issues, to specific social or interest groups, my aim is to make it easier to communicate and deal with various questions which belong to these issues. Another objection that can be made is that a “relevant social science paradigm” is a vague concept. The implication of the term paradigm is elusive. Margaret Masterman points out in “The Nature of Paradigm” in Lakatos (1970) that “the initial difficulty” is Thomas S. Kuhn’s many definitions of the term paradigm. When the term is linked to what is relevant it becomes even more diffuse.

THE CODING OF SUBSYSTEMS ACCORDING TO THE SIMULATION PROGRAM

The basic structure of the coding of subsystems is set out in *Figure 12:15* below. The notation of a critical subsystem starts with a letter (the simulation program does not allow that the code begin with a figure) for example, L to signify the subsystem in which a process takes place. L is then followed by the code (according to LS) which indicates the critical subsystem, for example, L328-9 (the subsystem supporter). The figure after the hyphen states the level (in this case the Earth). The inflow to and outflow from a subsystem are illustrated by means of the arrows which are marked with a code that commences with the letter R (Rates). Inflow ends with the figure. 1 and outflow with figure 2. Each inflow and outflow has also been assigned a code that links it with its critical subsystem supporter, R328-91 and R328-92 respectively.

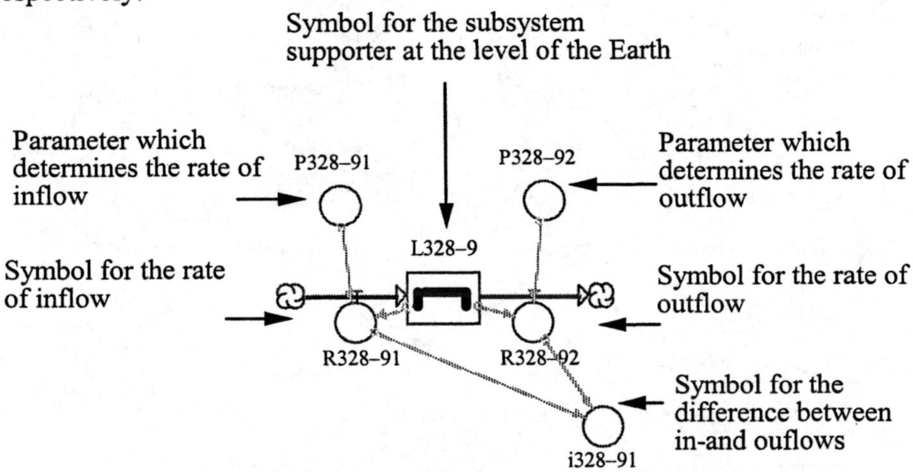

Figure 12:15 The basic coding of subsystems

The coding of parameters, which can be represented as a percentage change per unit of time using a code notation starting with P, is performed in the same way. The difference between in- and outflows is coded iL328-9.

Figure 12:16 shows a general description of the Earth according to the program in STELLA. The figure is equivalent to *Figure 12:2* with the symbols.

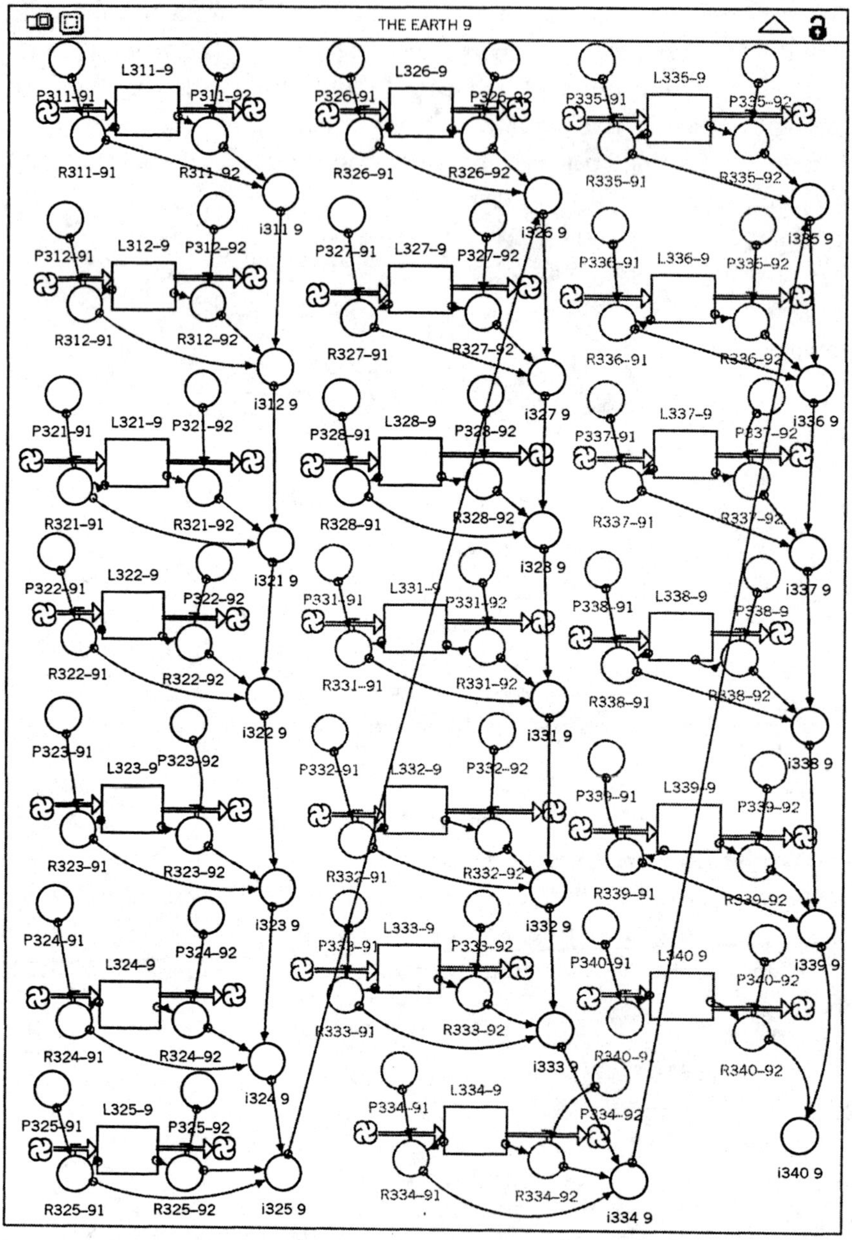

Figure12:16 is Figure 12:2 converted to the STELLA program at the level of the Earth. Subsystems are connected by an information system. Source T. Frandberg 1991.

Each system from the level of the cell to that of the Earth has been coded with a number from 1 (the cell) to 9 (the Earth).

The Earth's (level 9) reproducer (population) is coded L311-9 with R311-91 denoting inflow and R311-92 denoting outflow.

The parameter which is connected with the rate is denoted P311-92

A second number behind L311-91 indicates a component of the subsystem and a third figure different sizes of that component.

An example is shown in *Figure 12:17* below. The components of a subsystem in show amount of population in; low income economies L311-91, lower middle income economies L311-92, middle income economies L311-93, upper middle income ecomomies L311-94, and high income economies L311-95. The differences between inflow and outflow of a subsystem are connected to each other in order to build an information system. The differences which relate to L311-91 are denoted iL311-91. In this way the rate of inflow to the total subsystem can be determined and the overall figure for the subsystem in question can be calculated.

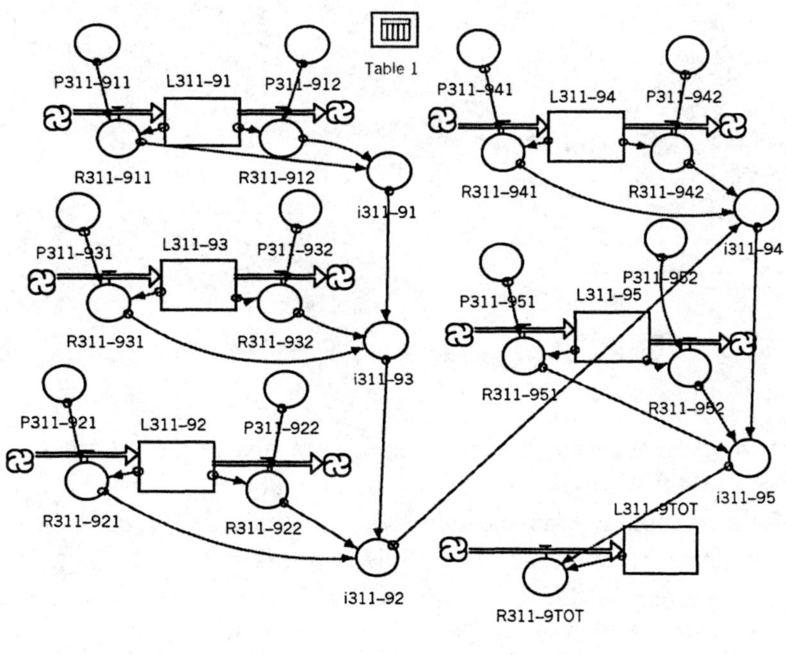

Figure 12:17 Shows subsystems of subsystem L311-9. (From plan to market. World development report 1994. page 194).

The result of the simulation can be shown in either tabular form or in a diagram.

L311-91	L311-94	L311-95	L311-9TOT	R311-9TOT	
In 2.10	0.47	0.85	5.60		
1	2.14	0.48	0.86	6.09	0.48
2	2.18	0.49	0.86	6.62	0.54
3	2.22	0.50	0.87	7.21	0.59

Table 1 shows results in tabular form.

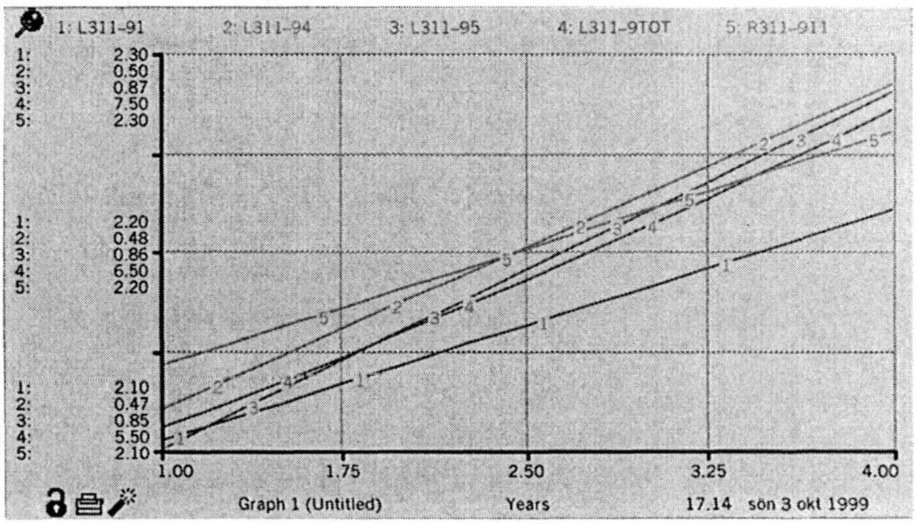

Diagram 1 shows results in a diagrammatic form.

The program has a great advantage in that the relations between subsystems and flows expressed in equations can be shown graphically. In the case of the community an extruder can for example be described as the exhaust systems of road vehicles, while at the same level examples of an extruder subsystem in this simulation are rubbish tips and sewage treatment works.

The decider is the only critical subsystem which cannot be parasitically or symbiotically dispersed to another system. Everything it controls must, by definition, be a subsystem or a component of its level. There is discussion as to how decider can be seen at the level of the Earth. An example of the component combination can be seen in *Figures 12:3, 12:4,* and *12:5.*

A subsystem such as decider, can have several "echelons" — for example five echelons as is in principle described in Stafford Beer (1979).

The program does not permit the rectangles that represent subsystems to be replaced by the symbol for the subsystem to which they belong. This means that one is obliged to use the above numerical code indicated in Living Systems in order to encode the pages which in STELLA symbolize critical subsystems.

Another reason why coding must take place is that the same symbols appear in the nine levels the cell – the Earth.

A third obstacle is that when a subsystem has several components the symbols cannot be appropriately coded in order to distinguish them from one another.

The symbols would furthermore be difficult to use when transcribing tables and diagrams, and they cannot be used when equations are to be written.

The results of the simulation can be transferred to other programs for example, to mathematical programs which permit more precise statistical mathematical treatment, or to programs which enable changes to be described in different ways such as Excel gas.

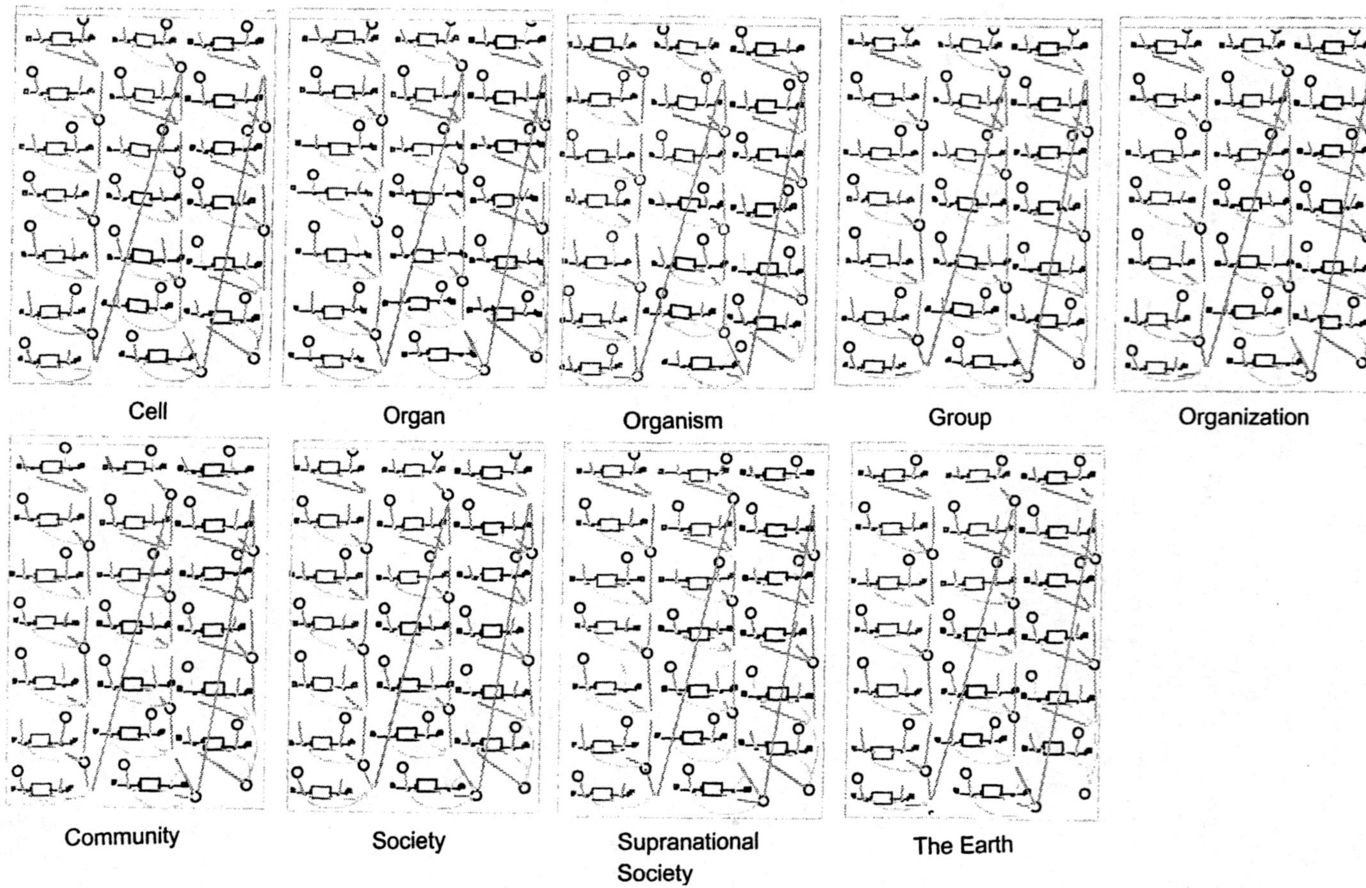

Figure 12:18 shows an overview of the nine levels and their subsystems. It is based on Figure 12:16 which shows subsystems at one level.

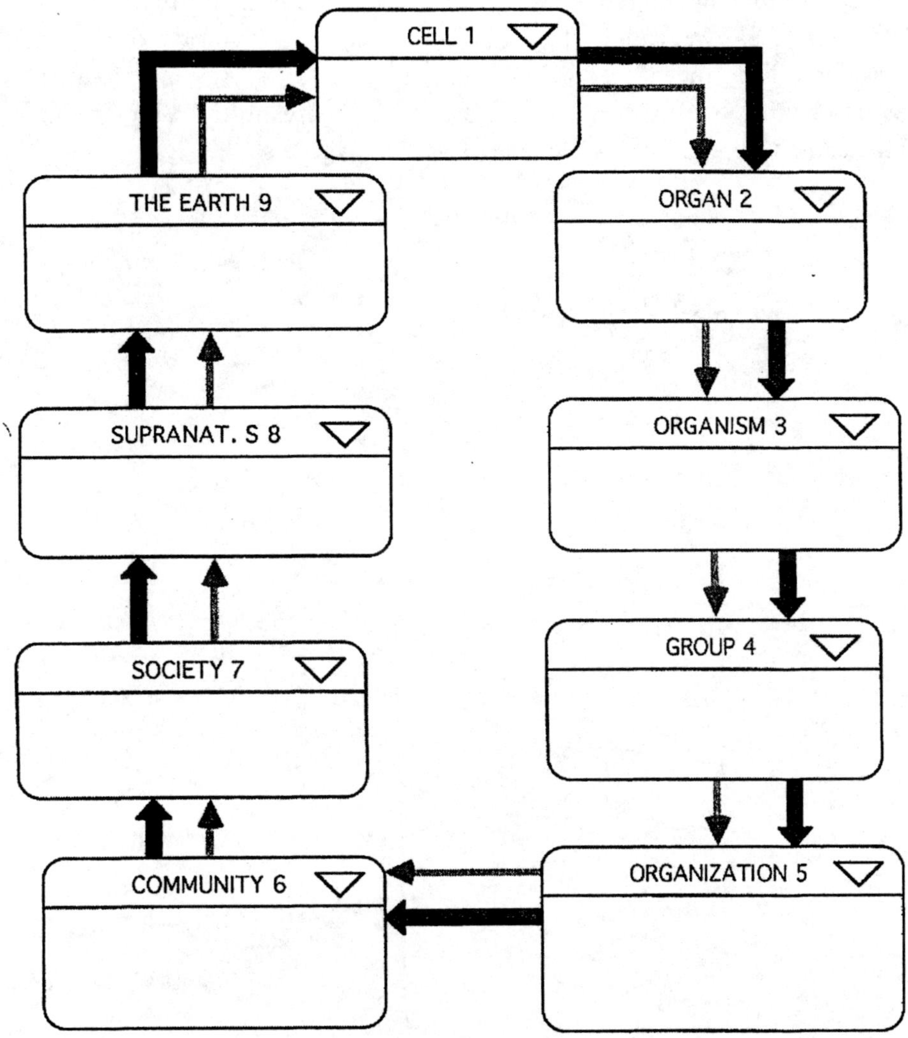

Figure 12:19 shows an overview of the nine levels. The simulation program has the possibility to easily transform subsystems in Figure 12:18 into this overview. By double-clicking on the arrows between the levels it is show which subsystems between the levels which are being studied and connected. The broad arrows show connection between matter-energy subsystems and the fine arrows connections between information subsystems. such as flows and parameters. Arrows can also simultaneously be drawn in the opposite direction.

The following pages present an example of quantification of the subsystem 311 (reproducer), 323 (converter), 324 (producer, and 326 (extruder). The Internet address where data is stated within pictures. By double-clicking on the table symbol the actual figures in the table are shown. In the same way a graph symbol shows actual diagrams.

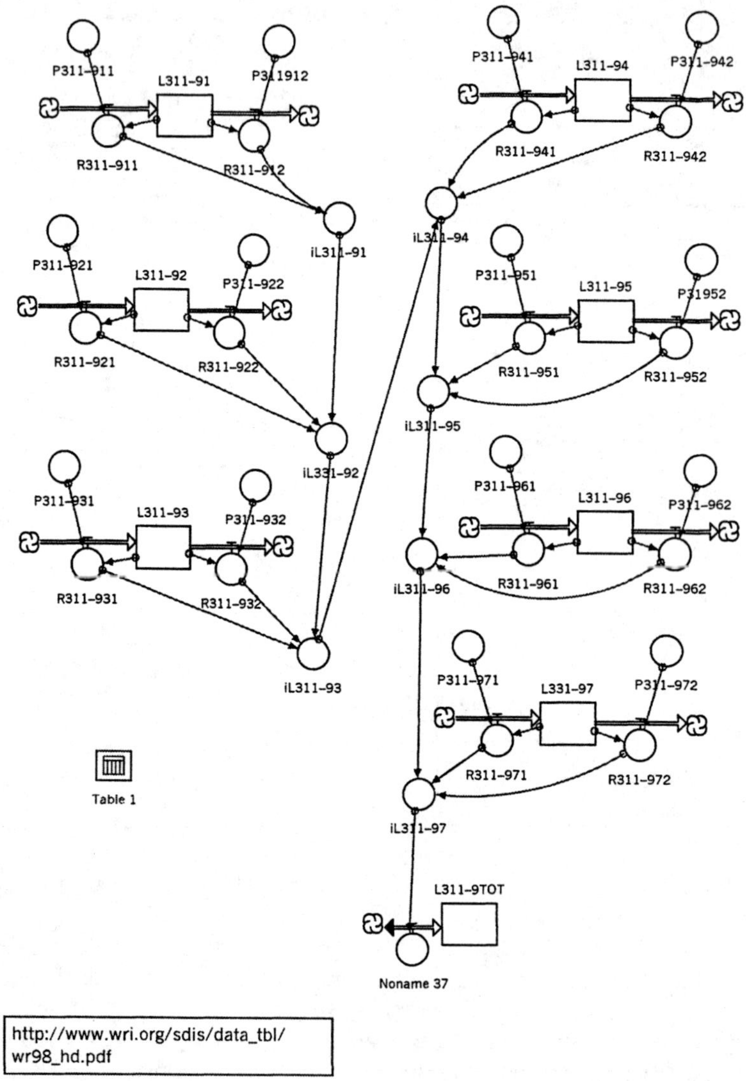

Figure 12:20 shows subsystem at level 311-9

World Resources 1998-99 **Chapter 7** **Popoulation and Development** **Data Table 7.1** **Size and Growth of Population and labor Force 1950-2050** **Central America**

Figure 12:21 shows how each subsystem (is documented. by the program) by means of a double-click on the subsystem symbol In this case 311-93.

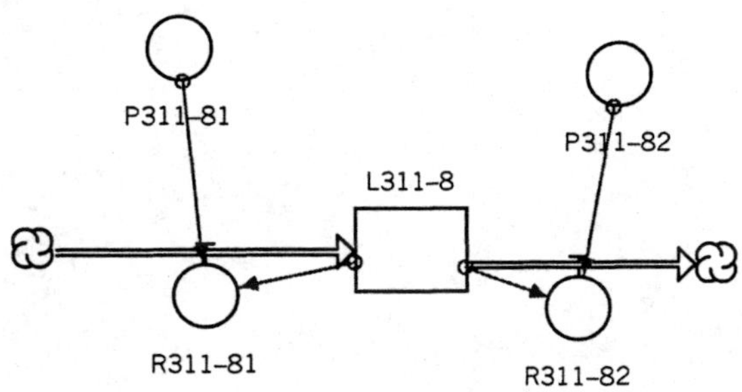

http:// www.oecd.org/publications/figures/index.htm e_06-07_demography.pdf

Figure 12:22 shows subsystem 311-8

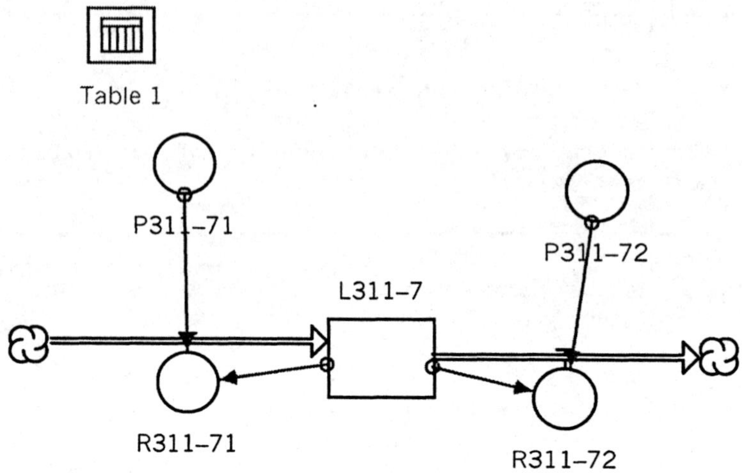

http://www.census.gov/cgi-bin/ipc/idbsum

Figure 12:23 shows subsystem 311-8

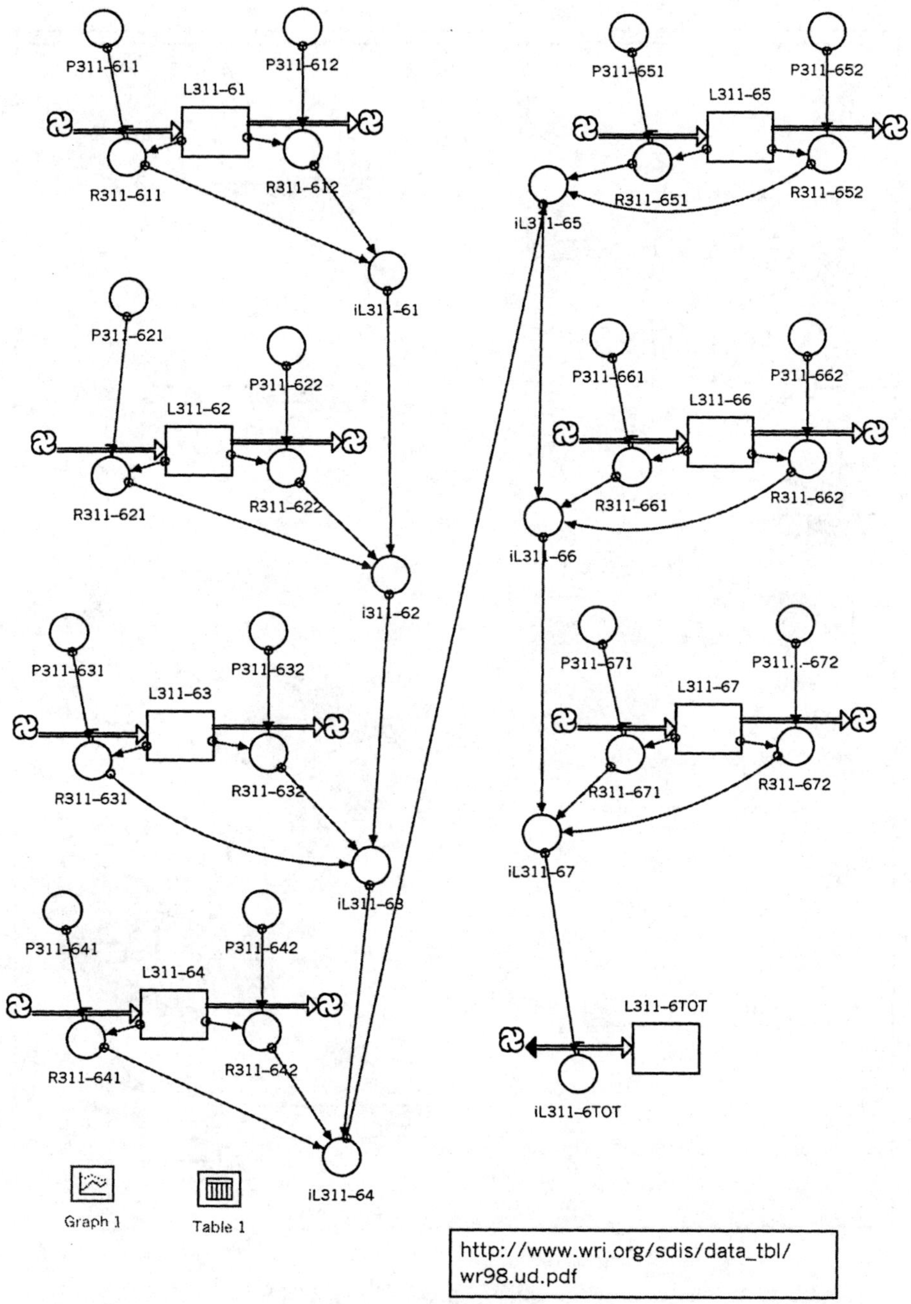

Figure 12:24 shows subsystem 311-6

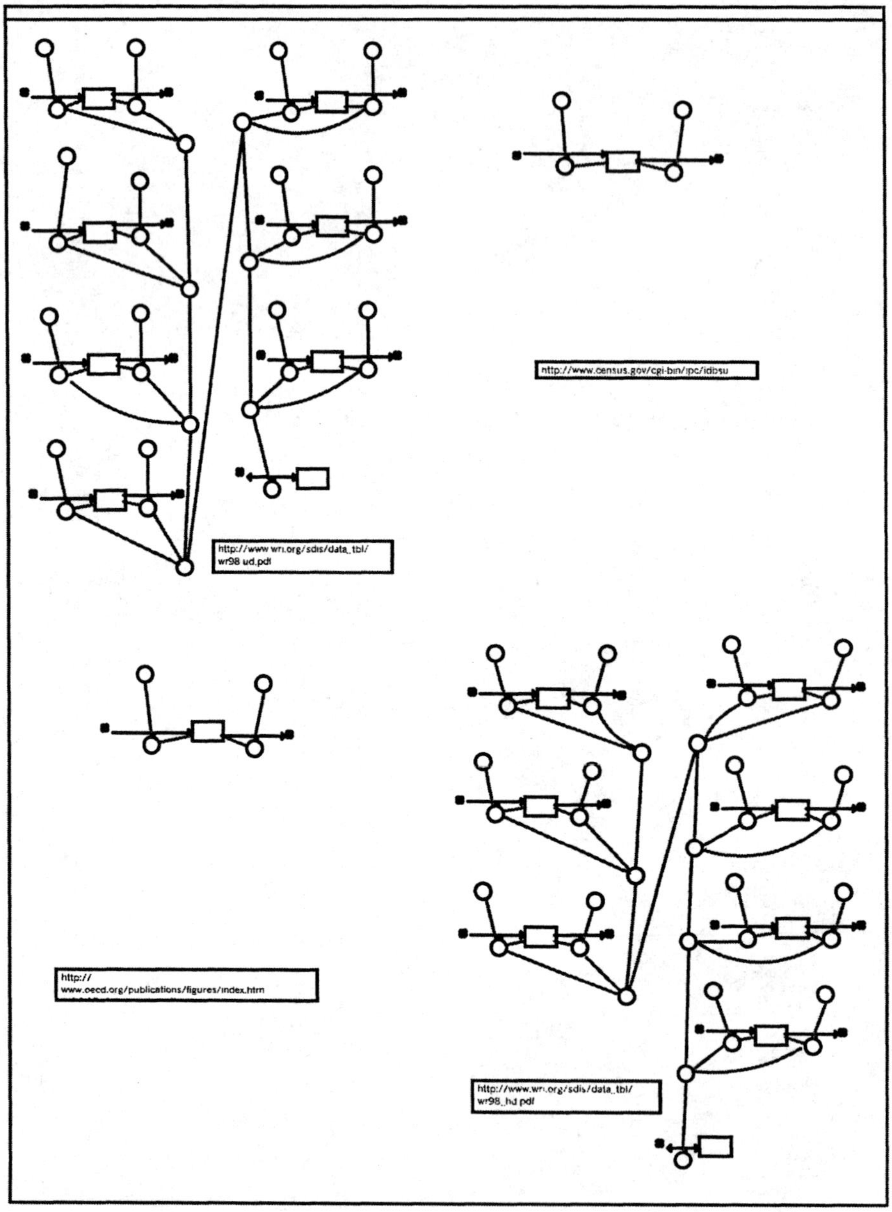

Figure 12:25 shows how the subsystems L311-6, L311-7, L311-8, L311-9 can be described by an overview. This is one third of 100% scale

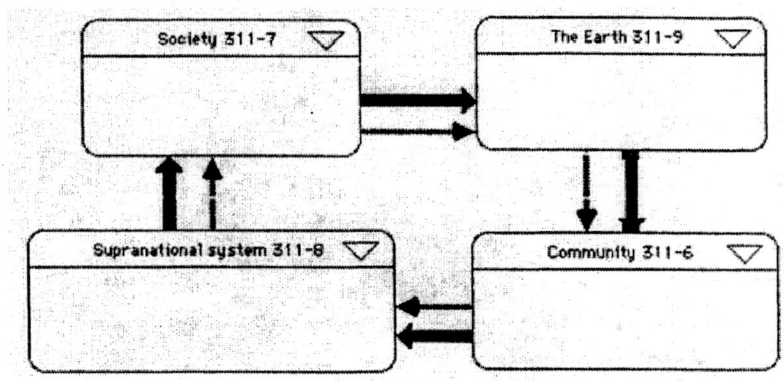

Figure 12:26 shows the above subsystems 311-9, 311-8, 311-7, and 311-6 in an overview which can form a basis for describing interactions.

Init.	L311-6	L311-7	L311-8	L311-9
0	2 865 724,00	274 943,00	1 093 792,00	5 892 904,00
1	2 927 964,55	277 142,54	1 100 354,75	5 964 523,43
2	2 991 944,85	279 359,68	1 106 956,88	6 037 256,16
3	3 057 717,76	281 594,56	1 113 598,62	6 111 121,93
4	3 125 337,85	283 847,32	1 120 280,21	6 186 140,90

Table 2 shows results of a simulation of subsystems 311-6, 311-7, 311,8, 311,9.

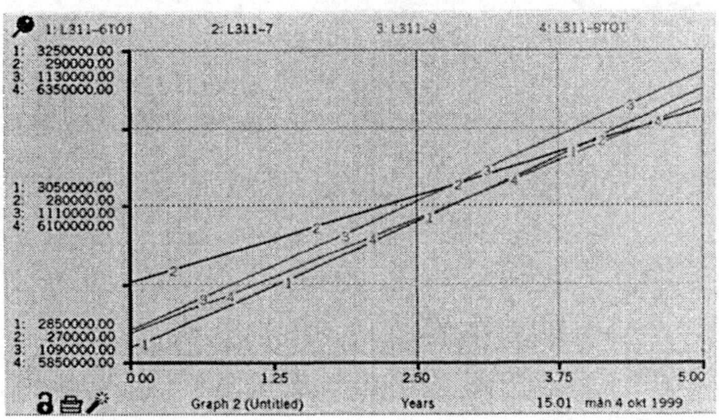

Diagram 2 shows the result in a diagrammatic form.

Further illustrations of urban population growth can for example be shown in the following diagrams

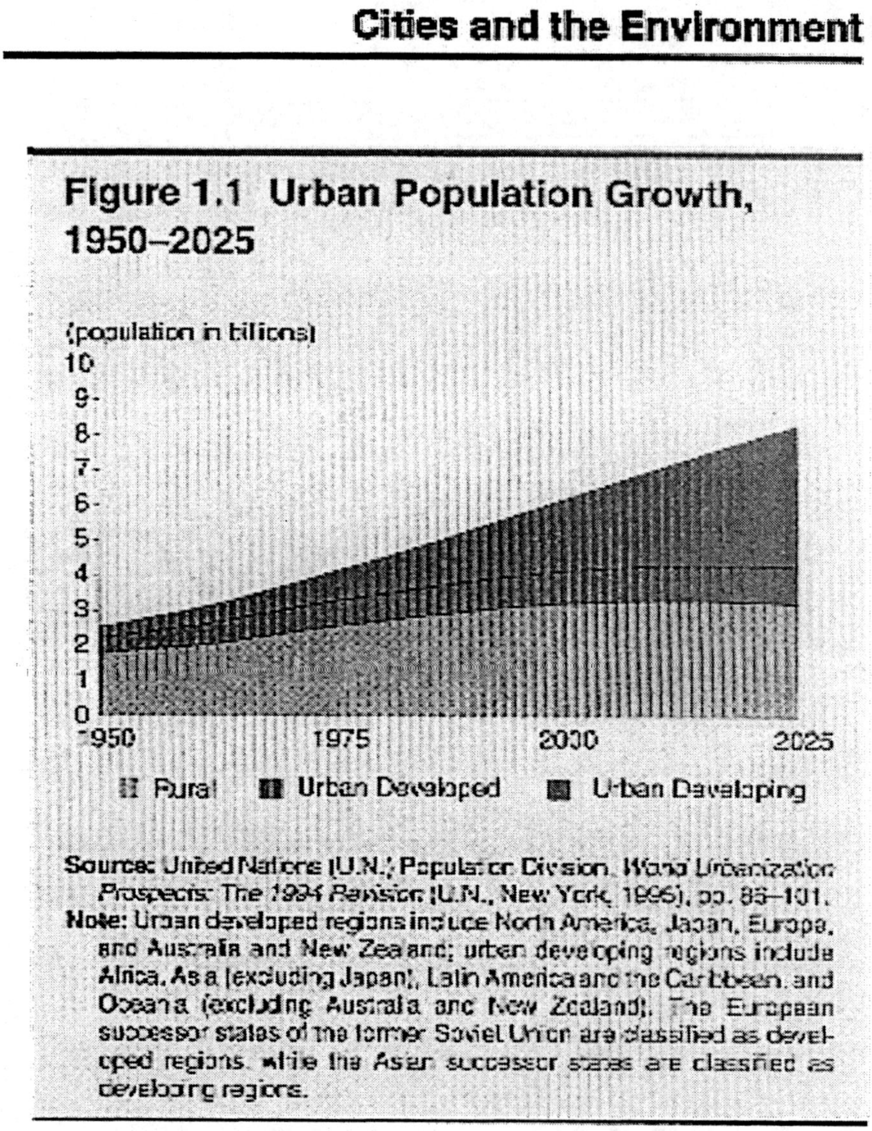

Diagram 3 The World Bank 1996, (p. 3)."World Resources. The Urban environment 1996-1997" 1996. Oxford University Press

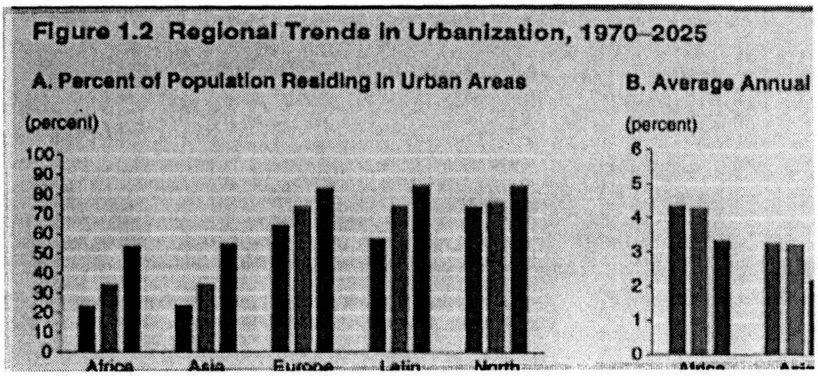

Diagram 4 The World Bank 1996, (p. 3)."World Resources. The Urban environment 1996-1997" 1996. Oxford University Press

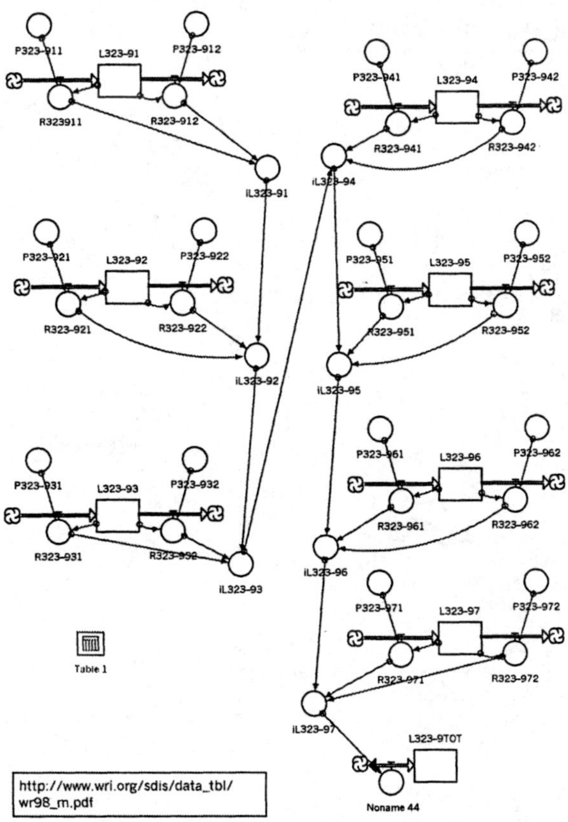

Figure12:27 shows how the subsystem 323-9 at level 9 can be described

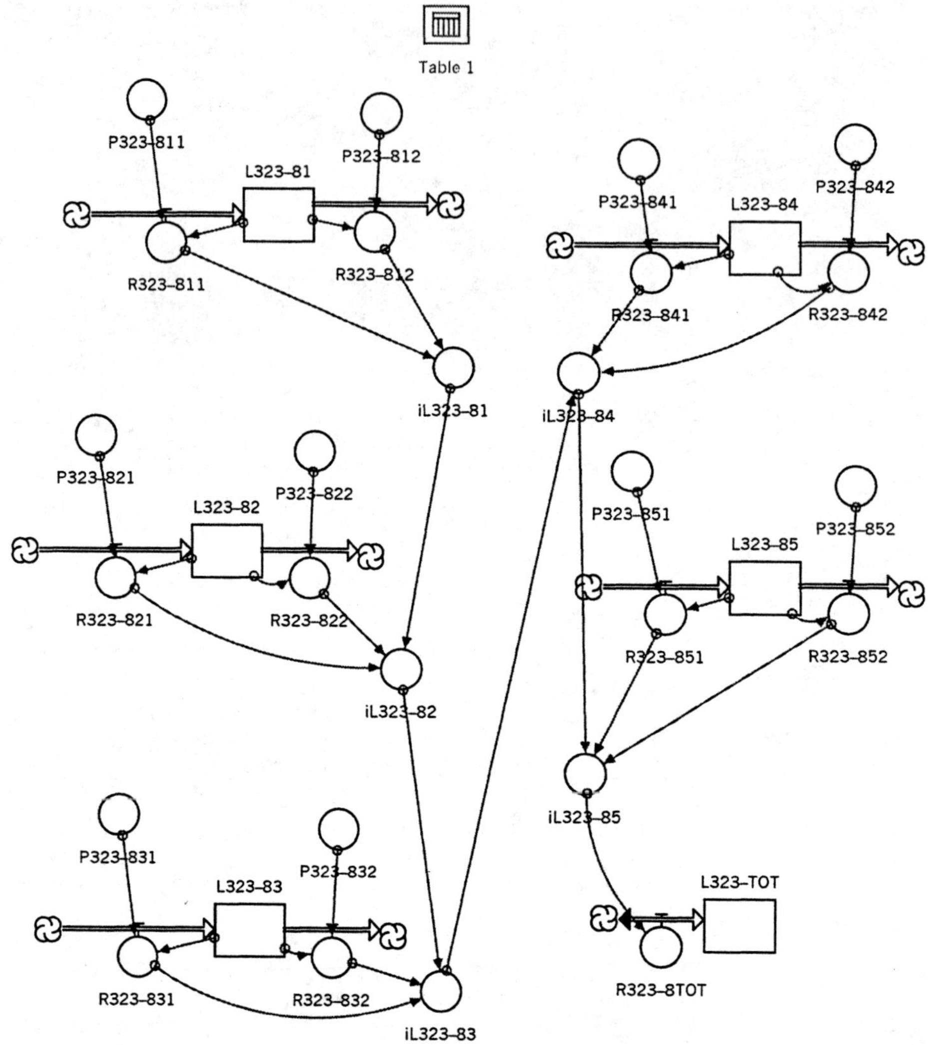

http://www.oecd.org/publications/figures/
e-42-43energy.prod.pdf

Figure 12:28 shows how the subsystem 323-7 can be described at this level

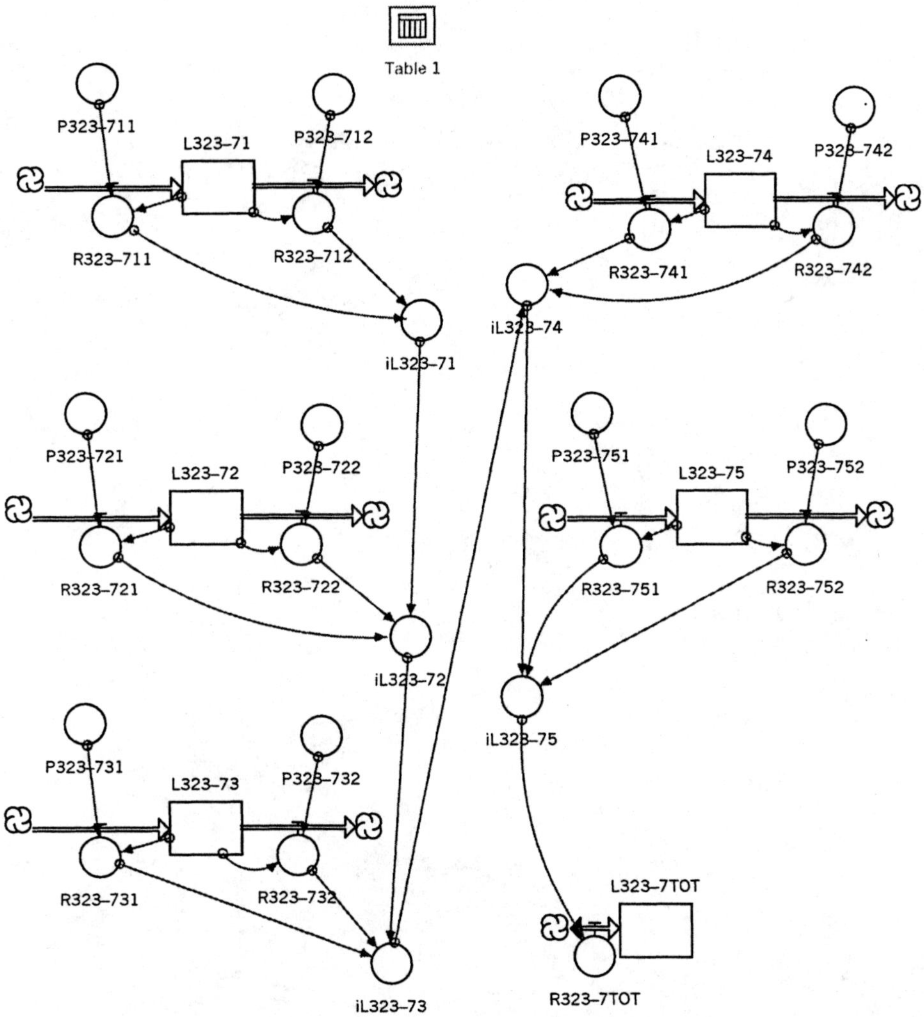

http://www.oecd.org/publications/figures/
e-42-43energy.prod.pdf

Figure 12:29 shows how the subsystem 323-7 can be described at this level

Data at level 323–6 has not yet been available

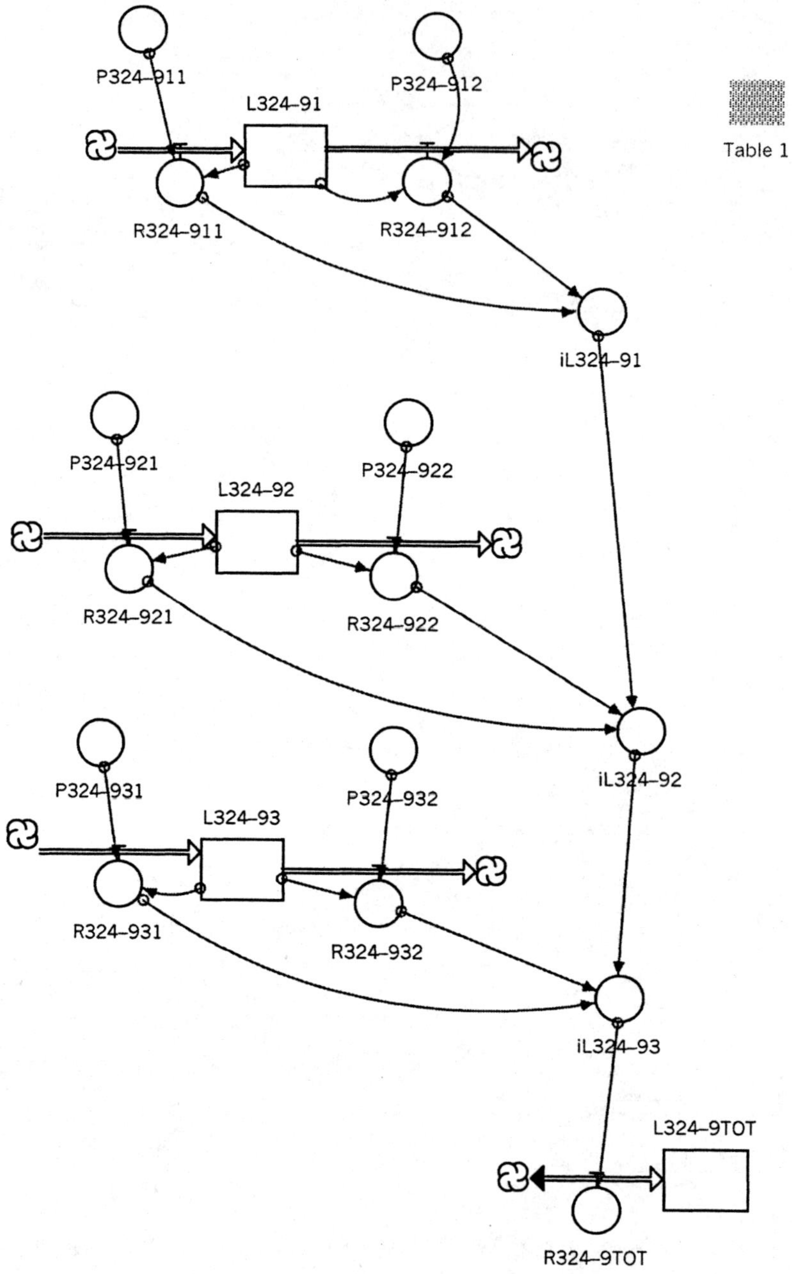

Figure 12:30 shows how subsystem 324-9 can be described at this level

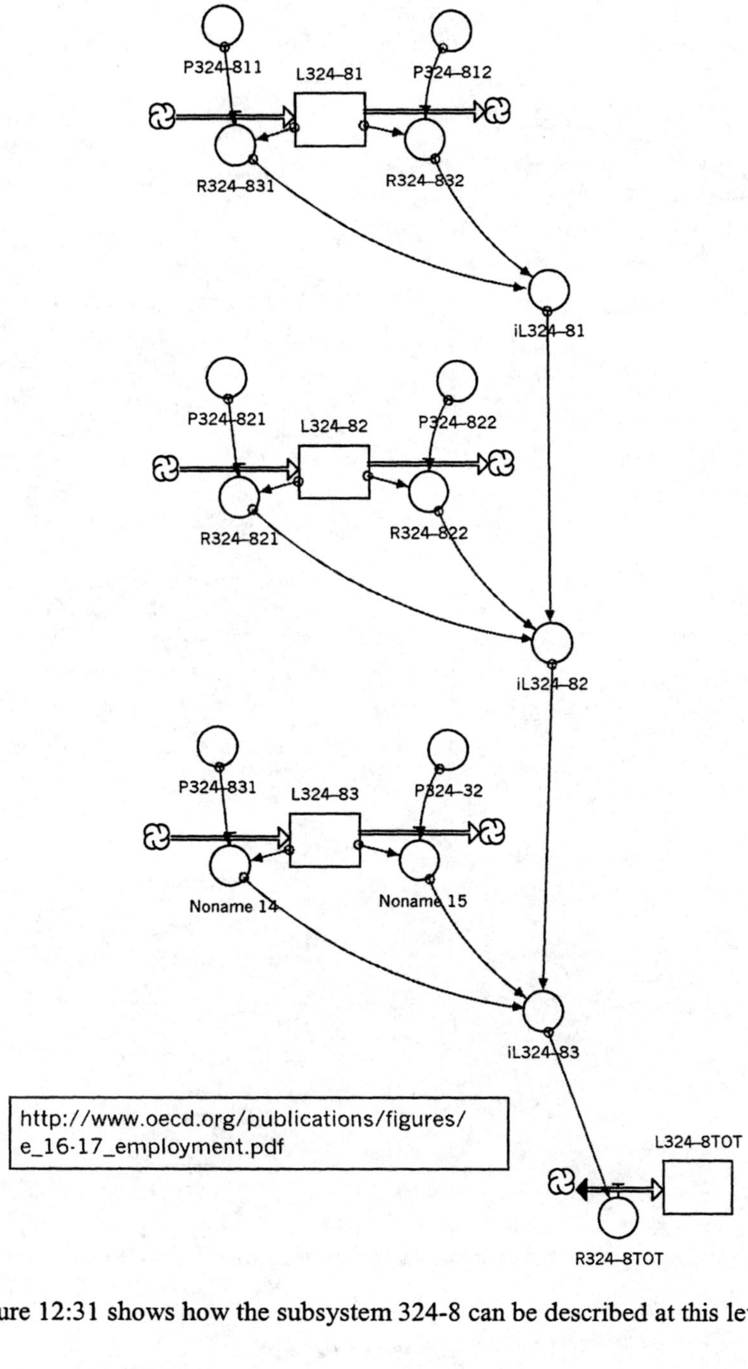

Figure 12:31 shows how the subsystem 324-8 can be described at this level

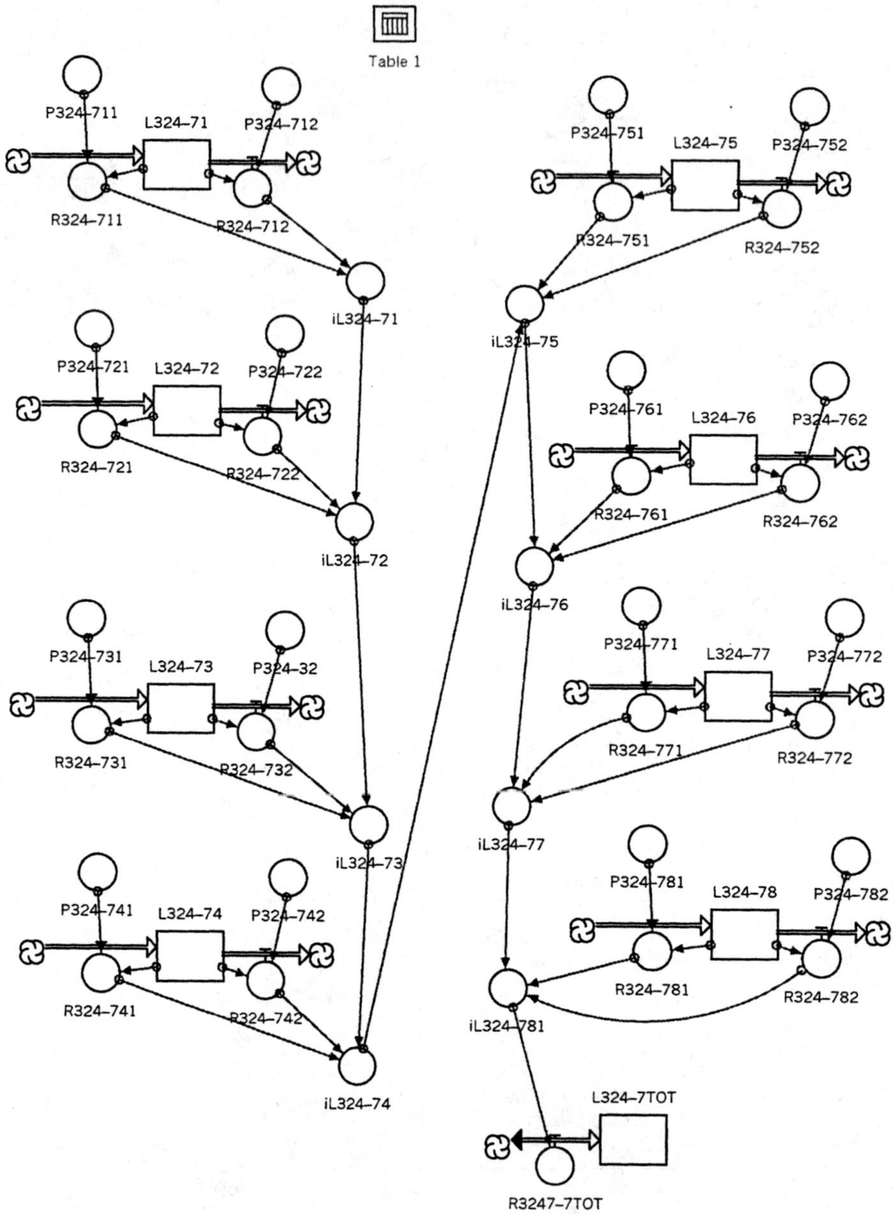

Figure 12:32 shows the subsystem at L324-7

Data at level 324-6 has not yet been available

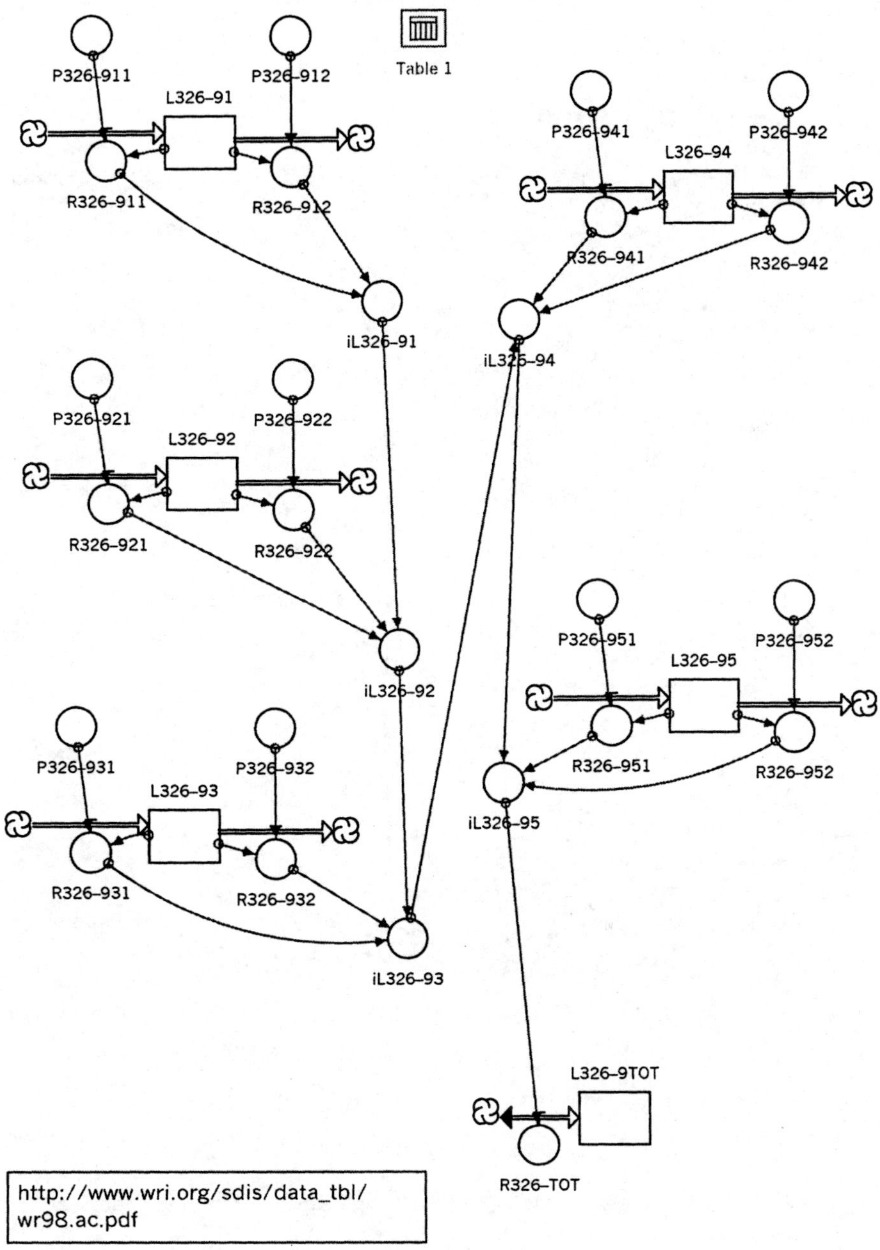

Figure 12:33 shows how the subsystem 326-9 can be described at this level

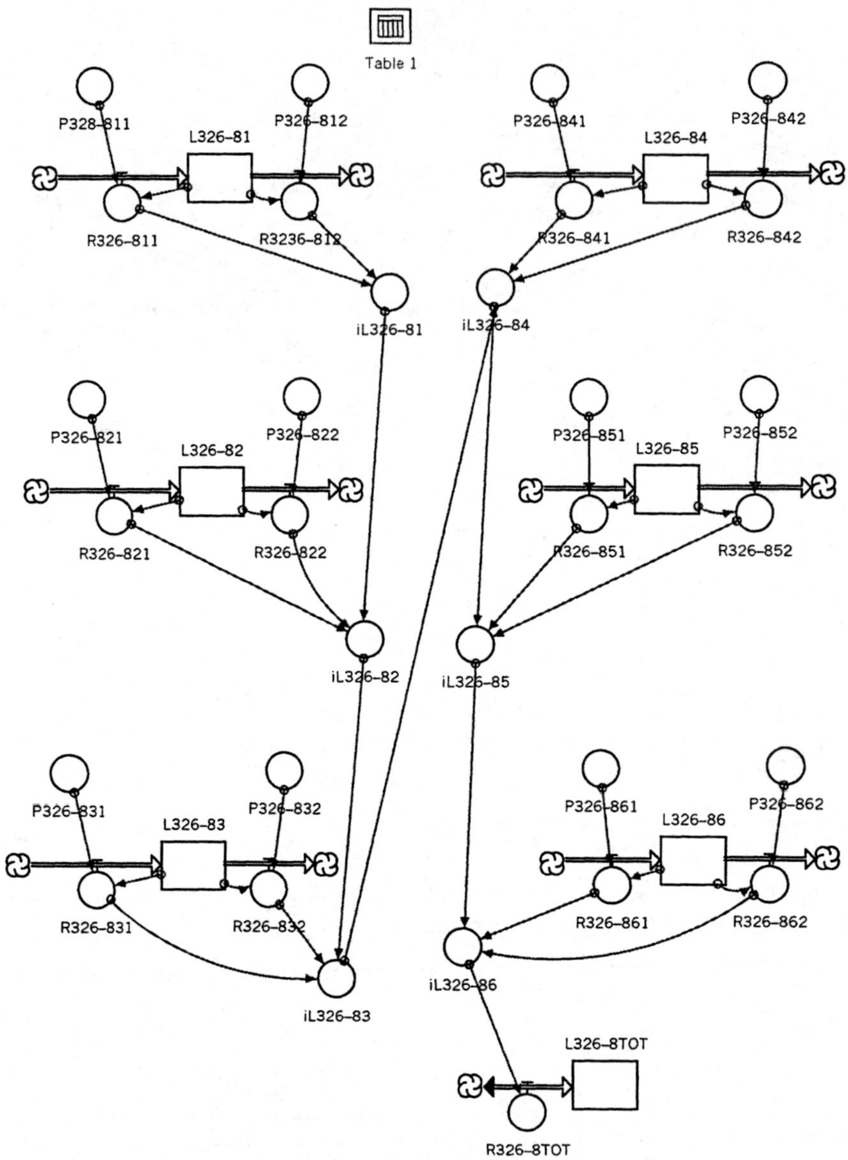

Figure 12:34 shows how subsystem 326-8 at this level can be described

Data for 326-7 has not yet been available

Data for 326-6 has not yet been available

CONCLUSION

The compilation of examples above portrays an application of the theory of Living Systems. It points to the possibility of firstly describing subsystems at one level and the bringing together, analysing, and reviewing subsystems at several levels, and study co-variations between them. This in turn will make it possible to see general qualities of subsystems within a particular level and at different levels. In this way a common frame of reference is created which in a joint project can give good possibilities for advocates of different subject areas to communicate their knowledge. One can then avoid the difficulty of communication when a project is described in terms of different subject areas with their own particular structures. In such cases a project can end in a compromise which satisfies individual subject areas but does then not conform to the aim of the project. That being said, the aim here is not to limit the expression of different subject areas but provide a possible framework for co-operation. Living Systems sees our portraying of reality outgoing from concrete systems which by means of conceptual systems result in abstracted systems. In this way we recognize reality which can be said to be similar to what in Kline (1995) is represented by "sysrep".

SUMMARY

At the same time as the boundaries of our areas of knowledge are moving even further out at macro and micro levels, assuming what for a layman are incomprehensible dimensions, we cannot see where the boundary for the total area of our knowledge goes. Kline (1995) illustrates in his figure that our knowledge lies between two unknown areas. We can as Peter Nilsson (1992 and 1993) assume that our thoughts, as well as energy and matter, are related to what came into existence after the big bang. This is in contrast to those who can not see a resemblance between our thinking and the primary cause before matter was formed. If we wish to understand these interrelations otherwise than in terms of interaction we ought to stand aside and observe the course of events, and not be a part of the result of the primary event. We can portray our environment and ourselves but we are lacking a firm point to which we can relate.

In different ways we search to structure and define the boundaries of what we see and know. This process is part of the development of man. Today we can follow how the time before the flourishing of Greek philosophy has had a great influence, and observe the great influence which Greek philosophy still has.

The world of medieval learning dealt with differences between our ways of looking at our environment. A difference prevailed between nominalists and empiricists and this discussion is of current interest. Alfred N. Whitehead embraces in his philosophy a view which can be characterized as objectivism in contrast to the viewpoint which does not see relations between observed objects as representing reality but as a process within the human brain. A middle course could be a point of view where the result is seen as a result of a co-operation between an objective (however that might be defined) observation and an interpretation which is assumed to be a result of subjective opinion. Living systems sees our portrayal of reality as having its departure point in concrete systems which by means of conceptual systems result in abstracted systems. This interpretation of how we recognise can be said to be similar to what in Kline (1995) is represented by "sysrep"

Unlike earlier years when the problem was that a major part of the work was to collect as much relevant information (data) as possible, we are today in a situation where we must choose the information (data) from an overwhelming information flow — an information flow which in some way must be surveyed, structured, and analysed. We also need to find qualities and connections which can be generally described at different levels. One tool for this is systems thinking. In previous chapters comparisons have been made between different aspects of systems, and different ways of designing models, and I have given suggestions as to how to collect information and how to process and analyse this information. I have then gone on to find that Living Systems is a theory which gives examples of applications which can form a basis for further studies of systems.

The possibility to collect information (data) via the Internet is a major advantage compared to retrieving of information at libraries or locally situated statistical sources. Warfield writes that reports written with availability to the same data can produce different results. It is consequently important that the data applied are easily retrievable and can easily be verified, in order to avoid a situation where different results are dependent on the use of different data in the same reports.

The application of the program STELLA gives possibilities to explicit as well as in detail portray the structures of the system, its structure and its equations and the graphical figures which these equations represent. There is also the possibility of transferring and showing results with the help of other programs, for example Excel.

To sum up: the results of simulation effected according to Living Systems should primarily be seen as an aid to co-operation and increased understanding between the representatives of different subject areas and areas of interest.

REFERENCES

Auger, Pierre. 1989. *Dynamics and Thermodynamics in Hierarchically Organized Systems.* Pergamon Press, New York, USA.

Aulin, Arvid. 1989. *Foundations of Mathematical Systems Dynamics.* Pergamon Press, New York, USA.

Ayres, Robert U. 1978. *Resources, Environment & Economics.* Wiley & Sons Publication, New York, USA.

Bailey, Kenneth, D. 1990 "*Social Entropy Theory*". State University of New York Press, Albany

Bailey, Kenneth. D. *Sociology and the New Systems Theory. Toward a Theoretical Synthesis.* State University of New York Press, Albany, 1994 pp. 25, 70, 157 199, 201.

Bateson, Gregory. 1979. *Mind and Nature A necessary unit.* William Collins Sons & Co., Ltd. Glasgow, Great Britain.

Beer, Stafford. 1973. *The World We Manage.* Behavioral Science Vol. 18, No. 3, May, 1973.

Beer, Stafford. 1979. *The Heart of Enterprise.* John Wiley & Sons, New York, USA. Collected from Beer (1979), Churchman (1982) and Campbell (1981).

Beer, Stafford. 1979. *The Heart of Enterprise.* John Wiley & Sons, New York, USA. One person who points to the importance of regarding the Earth as a level is Stafford Beer in his Banquet Address to the Silver Jubilee Meeting on Operational Research and the Social Sciences, Queen's College, Cambridge, April 12, 1989.

Behavioral Science vol.24, No.4, May 1974.

Behavioral Science. Vol. no. 18. No. 3, may, 1973. Journal of the Society for 1973 General Systems Research. University of Louisville, Louisville, Kentucky, USA.

Bernstein Richard J. 1976. *The restructuring of social and political theory.* Basil Blackwell. Oxford, United Kingdom.

Blalock, Hubert M. Jr. 1964. *Causal Inferences in Nonexperimental Research.* The University of North Carolina Press, North Carolina State University Print Shop, USA.

Bobrow, Daniel G. 1985. *Qualitative Reasoning about Physical Systems* The MIT Press, Cambridge, Massachusetts, USA.

Bohm, David and F. David Peat. 1987. *Science, Order and Creativity.* Bantam Books, New York, USA.

Boulding, Kenneth E. 1978. *Ecodynamics.* Sage Publications, Beverly Hills California, USA.

Boulding, Kenneth E., Stahr, Elvis J., Fabricant, Solomon, Gainsbrugh, Martin R. 1971. *Economics of Pollution.* New York University Press, New York, USA.

Briggs, John & F. David Peat. 1990. *Turbulent Mirror. An Illustrated Guide to Chaos Theory and the Science of Wholeness.* Harper & Row Publishers, New York, USA.

Broad C. D. 1925. *The Mind and its Place in Nature.* Routledge & Kegan Paul, London, England. Reprinted 1980.

Bronowski, J. 1965. *The Identity of Man.* Ed 1971. American Museum Science Books, New York, USA.

Bunge, Mario. 1973. *Method, Model and Matter.* Kluwer Academic Publishers, Dordrecht, The Netherlands.

Bunge, Mario. 1989. *Ethics: The Good and the Right. Treatise on basic Philosophy.* Vol. 8. Kluwer Academic Publishers, Dordrecht, The Netherlands.

Campell, Tom. 1981. *Seven Theories of Human Society.* Clarendon Press, Oxford, England.

Capra, Fritiof. 1982. *The Turning Point. Science, Society, and the Rising Culture.* Wildwood House, London, England.

Caws, Peter. 1989. *The Law of Quality and Quantity, or what Numbers can and can't describe. The Qualitative-Quantitative Distinction in the Social Sciences.* Edited by Barry Glassner and Jonathan D. Moreno. Kluwer Academic Publishers. Dordrecht. The Netherlands.

Cellier, Francois E. 1982. *Progress in Modelling and Simulation.* Academic Press, New York, USA.

Churchland, Paul M. 1988. *Matter and Consciousness.* The MIT Press, Cambridge, Massachusetts, USA.

Churchman, C. West Churcman. 1982. *Thought and Wisdom.* Intersystems Publications, Seaside, California.

Constanca, Robert. 1991. *Ecological Economics. The Science and Management of Sustainability.* Columbia University Press,

Corning, Peter A. and Kline Stephen Jay. 1998 "Thermodynamics, Information and Life Revisited, Part 1: 'To Be or Entropy'. Systems Research and Behavioral Science. Volume 15 Number 4.

Corning, Peter A. and Kline Stephen Jay. 1998 "Thermodynamics, Information and Life Revisited, Part 1: 'To Be or Entropy'. *Systems Research and Behavioral Science. Volume 15 Number 4*

Corning,Peter. 1998. *Systems Research and Behavioral Science Vol 15 Number 6 Nov.-Dec.* p. 455 After having read Peter A. Corning's and Stephen Jay Kline's article "Thermodynamics, Information and Life Revisited, Part 1: 'To Be or Entropy' in Systems Research?

De Duve, Christian. 1984. *A Guided Tour of the Living Cell.* Volume 1 and 2. Scientific American Books, Inc. New York, USA.

De Duve, Christian. 1984. *A Guided Tour of the Living Cell.* Volume 1 and 2. Scientific American Books, Inc. New York, USA.

De Greene, Kenyon B. 1973. *Sociotechnical Systems. Factors in Analysis,Design, and Management.* Prentice-Hall, Inc. Englewood Cliffs, New Jersey, USA.

Dewey, Edward R. 1985. *Cyklerna- kretsloppen.* Title of the original: *Cycles. The Mysterious Forces that Trigger Events.* Liber Förlag, Lund, Sweden.

Emery F. E. 1969. *Systems Thinking.* Penguin Books Ltd. Harmondsworth, Middlesex, England

Eriksson, Karl-Erik & Kristian Lindgren & Bengt Å. Månsson. 1987. *Structure, Context, Complexity, Organization.* World Scientific Singapore, Malaysia.

Estey, James, Arthur. 1964. *Business Cycles. Their Nature, Cause and Control.* Fifth printing. Prentice-Hall Inc., New York, USA.

Flood, Robert L., Jackson, Michael C. 1991. *Creative Problem Solving – Total Systems Intervention.* John Wiley & Sons Ltd, Chichester, England.

Ford, Lewis S. and Kline, George L. 1983 *Explorations in Whitehead's Philosophy.* New York: Fordham University Press.

Forrester (1969), and Forrester (1973).

Forrester, Jay, W. 1969. *Urban Dynamics.* Systems Practice. The MIT Press, Massachusetts, USA.

Frandberg, Tage. Living Systems: 1995.*Simulation Studies at the Level of Society.* Presented at the International Conference "Problems of Excavating Cybernetics and Systems". Centre for Innovation and Co-operative Technology. Amsterdam.

Frandberg, Tage. *Living Systems: Simulation Studies at the Level of the Earth.* ISSS meeting July 1995 in Amsterdam, 1995 a.

Frandberg, Tage.*Environmental and Systems Thinking-Simulation Studies of Living Systems.* Thesis. Royal Institute of Technology. Stockholm, Sweden. 1994. p. 126

FRN. Källa/28. 1987. *The Threat of the Ozone is Unexpectedly Great.* (in Swedish). Forskningsrådsnämnden, Stockholm, Sweden.

Funtowitz and Ravetz (p. 151):

Gell-Mann, Murray T*he Quark and the Jaguar* swedish edition 1997) ICA Bokförlag, Västerås, Sweden.

Georgescu-Roegen, Nicholas. 1971. *The Entropy Law and the Economic Process.* Harvard University Press. Cambridge, Massachusetts, USA

Georgescu-Roegen, Nicholas. 1972. *To Build an Economic Science after the Model of Mechanics.* Vanderbilt University Nashville U S A.

Gribbin, John. 1990. *Hothouse Earth, The Greenhouse Effect & Gaia.* Black Swan London, England.

Gustavsson, Bernt. 1988. *Worldviews. Views of Mankind, Society, and Nature.* (in Swedish) Wahlström & Widstrand, Stockholm, Sweden.

Hall, Charles A. S. 1992. *Economic Development or Developing Economics: What Are Our Priorities?* Ecosystem Rehabilitation, volume 1: Policy Issues edited by Mohan K. Wali, pp. 101-126. SPD Academic Publishing bv. The Hague, The Netherlands.

Hall, Charles A. S. and Day, John W. 1977. *Ecosystem Modeling in Theory and Practice.* University Press of Colorado. (reprinted 1990) Niwot, Colorado. USA.

Hardwick, Philip. 1986. *An Introduction to Modern Economics.* Longman, London, England.

Hawking, Stephen W. 1988. *A brief History of Time.* Bantam Books. London, England

Hawking, Stephen W. 1988. *A brief History of Time.* Bantam Books.London, England

Hermerén, Göran et al. 1981. *The Methodology of the KPP project, An Assessment of an Interdisciplinary experiment,* R11:19811981. (in Swedish) The Swedish Council of Building Research, Stockholm, Sweden.

Herrman, Heinz. 1989. *Cell Biology, An Inquiry into the Nature of the Living State.* Harper & Row Publishers, New York. USA.

Hershey, Daniel. 1986. *Ageing of Cities, Corporations and Civilizations.* Systems Research. Volume 3, Number 1, 1986. Pergamon Press, New York, USA.

Ho, Mae-Wan. *The Rainbow and the Worm. The Physics of Organisms.* Word Scientific Publishing Co Singapore, 1993 p. 174

Hopkins, Johns. 1966. *Environmental Quality in a Growing Economy.* The John Hopkins Press, Washington D. C. USA.

Horgan, John. *From Complexity to Perplexity.* Scientific American, Inc. New York. June 1995 pp. 74-79

Jackson, Michael. 1995 a, *Beyond the Fads: Systems Thinking for Managers.*Systems Research Vol. 12 No.1, pp. 25-42.

Jackson, Michael. 1996 b, *Contemporary Systems Thinking: Total Systems Intervention"* FOA Stockholm Sweden. 1996-05-08.

Jackson, Mike C. *Only Connect! An Annotated Bibliography Reflecting the Breadth and Diversity of Systems Thinking.* Systems Research,

Jackson, Tim. 1993. *Clean Production Strategies. Developing Preventive Environmental management in the Industrial Economy.* Lewis Publishers, London, England.

Johannisson, Karin. 1988. *The Measurable Society. Statistics and The Social Dream in 18th-Century Europe.* (in Swedish) Norstedts, Stockholm, Sweden.

Kirk, James. 1993. *Organicism as Reenchantment.* New York: Peter Lang

Klapp, Orrine E. 1973. *Models of Social Order.* National Press Books,Palo Alto. CA. USA.

Klapp, Orrine E. 1976. *Opening and Closing in Open Systems*. Behavioral Science. Journal of the Society for General Systems Research. Vol. 20 nr 4 July 1976. Louisville, Kentucky, USA. '

Kline, Stephen, Jay 1995 *Conceptual Foundations for Multidisciplinary Thinking* .(1995). Stanford University Press, Stanford, California.

Klir, George. 1985. *Architecture of Systems Problem Solving.* Plenum Press,New York, USA.

Krippendorff, Klaus. 1986. *A Dictionary of Cybernetics.* University of Pennsylvania, Philadelphia, USA.

Kvale (1987)

Kvale, Steinar. 1989. *Issues of Validity in Qualitative Research*Studentlitteratur, Lund, Sweden. Behavioral Science vol.24, No.4, May 1974.

Langefors, Börje. 1970. *Theoretical Analysis of Information Systems.* First Volume. Studentlitteratur, Lund, Sweden.

Langton, Christopher G. 1989. *Artificial Life.* Addison-Wesley Publishing Company, Inc., California, USA.

Langton, Christopher G. 1989. *Artificial Life.* Addison-Wesley Publishing Company, Inc., California, USA.

Laszlo, Ervin. *The Interconnected Universe. Conceptual foundations of Transdisciplinary Unified Theory.* Word Scientific Publishing Co Singapore, 1995. p. 141, 140

Leclerc, Ivor. 1961. *The Relevance of Whitehead.* London:George Allen & Unwin Ltd.

Lecomte Du Noüy. 1948. *The Road to Reason.* Longmans, Green and Co., New York, USA.

Levy, Steven. 1992. *Artificial Life The Quest for a New Creation.* Pantheon Books, New York, USA.

Lindahl Kiessling Kerstin ed. *Pitting knowledge in Struggle against Crisis.* (in Swedish). Kunskap i kamp mot kris. Natur och kultur. The Royal Swedish Academy of Sciences. Stockholm. 1996

Lovelock, James. 1988. *The Ages of Gaia. A Biography of Our Living Earth.* The Commonwealth Fund Book Program of Memorial Sloan- Kettering Cancer Center, New York, USA.

Lowe, Victor. 1990. *Alfred North Whitehead. The Man and his Work Volume II:1910-1947.* Baltimore: The John Hopkins University Press.

Lucas, George R. Jr. 1989. *The Rehabilitation of Whitehead* Albany: State University of New York Press

Lundqvist, Lars. 1983. *Methods for analysing and planning for building atransportation system.* Swedish council for Building Research, Stockholm, Sweden.

Mader, A. 1988. *A Transcription-Translation Activation Feedback Circuit as a Function of Protein Degradation, with the Quality of Protein Mass Adaption Related to the Average Functional Load.* Journal of Theoretical Biology, Volume 134, Number 2 17. September 1988. Academic Press, Harcourt Brace, Jovanovich, Publishers. London, England.

Margulis, Lynn and Sagan, Dorion.*What is Life?* Weidenfeld and Nicolson Ltd. The Orion Publishing Group. London, 1995.

Mayumi, K. 1991. *Georgescu-Roegen's "Fourth Law of Thermodynamics" and the Flow-Fund Model.* European Association for Bioeconomic Studies-E. A. B. S. 11 Via Larga-20122, Milano, Italy.

Meadows, Paul. 1957. Models, Systems and Science. *American Sociological Review.* Vol 22 Number 1 pp. 3-9

Miller, James, G. *Living systems.* Mc Graw-Hill Book Co. New York, 1978. Mikulecky, Donald C. 1983. *A Network Thermodynamic Approach to the Hill-King and Altman Approach to Kinetics: Computer simulation. Progress in Clinical and Biological Research.* Volume 126. Alan R. Liss, Inc. New York, USA.

Mitsch William J. and Sven Erik Jörgensen. 1989. *Ecological Engineering. An Introduction to Ecotechnology.* John Wiley & Sons, New York, USA.

Morgan, Gareth. 1986. *Images of Organization.* SAGE Publications, Inc., Beverly Hills, California. USA.

Mumford, Lewis. 1938. *The Culture of Cities* (in Swedish Stadskultur) Kooperativa Förbundets Förlag, Stockholm, Sweden.

Nagel, Ernest. 1961.*The Structure of Science.* Routledge and & Kegan Paul. Reprinted 1979, London, England.

Nagel, Thomas. 1986.*The View from Nowhere.* Oxford University Press, New York, USA.

New York, USA. Conrad, Michael. 1983. *Adaptability. The Significance of Variability from Molecule to Ecosystem.* Plenum Press, New York, USA.

Nicolis, Gregoire & Ilya Prigogine. 1989. *Exploring Complexity.* W.H. Freeman and Company, New York, USA.

Nilsson, Peter. 1992. *Rymdljus* (in Swedish) *Spacelight*. Månpocket, Norstedts förlag. Stockholm, Sweden.

Nilsson, Peter. 1993.Solvindar (in Swedish) Sunwinds. Månpocket, Norstedts förlag. Stockholm, Sweden.

Optner, Stanford L. 1965. *Systems Analysis for Business and Industrial. Problem Solving*. Prentice-Hall Inc. Englewood Cliffs, N.J., USA

Pagels, Heinz. 1988.*The Dreams of Reason*. Simon and Schuster, New York, USA.

Peccei, Aurelio & Ikeda, Daisaku. 1984. *Before it is to Late*. Kodansha, Tokyo, Japan.

Pilz, Anders.*Medeltidens lärda värld* (in Swedish) English orig. The World of Medieval Learning. Blackwell, Oxford 1981.

Popper Karl R. and Eccles John C. 1977. *The Self and Its Brain*.Springer Verlag, New York, USA.

Radetzki, Marian. 1990. *Growth and Environment*. (in Swedish). SNS förlag. Stockholm Sweden

Rose, Kenneth Jon. 1988. *The Body in Time*. John Wiley & Sons, Inc., New York, USA.

Rosen, Robert. 1991. *Life Itself. A Comprehensive Inquiry Into the Nature, Origin, and Fabrication of Life*. Columbia University Press, New York, USA.

Ryding Sven-Olof. 1992. *Environmental Management Handbook*. Lewis. Publishers, Boca Raton, Florida, USA.

Samuelson, Paul A. 1964. *Economics. An Introductory Analysis*. (Sixth Edition) McGraw-Hill Inc, (Thirteenth Edition 1989) New York, USA.

Samuelsson Kjell 1978 Samuelson, Kjell. 1978a.*Informatics by General Systems and Cybernetics*. The Royal Institute of Technology and the University of Stockholm. TRITA-IBADB-5011. Stockholm, Sweden.

Schrödinger, Erwin. 1944. *What is Life & Mind and Matter*. Cambridge University Press (Reprinted 1979), Cambridge, England.

Statens offentliga utredningar. 1984. *Political Goal of Health and demand planning of needs*. (in Swedish)*Hälsopolitiska mål och behovsbaserad planering. SOU 1984:40. (in Swedish)* Socialdepartementet, Stockholm, Sweden.

STELLA. 1994. High Performance Systems Inc Hanover U S A,

Swedish Council for Building Research. D6:1979. 1979. *Research Into Local Planning Processes.* A Report from a Colloquium in Sweden. Stockholm, Sweden.

The Natural Environment in Figures. 1987. *Official Statistics of Sweden. Stockholm, Sweden.*

Ulrich, Werner. 1983. *Critical Heuristics of Social Planing.* Verlag Paul Haupt Bern und Stuttgart. Printed in Switzerland

Umpleby, Stuart. 1990. *The Science of Cybernetics and the Cybernetics of Science.* Cybernetics and Systems: An International Journal 21:109-121 Hemisphere Publishing Corporation, Washington, USA.

Vandervert, L. R. 1990. *Systems Thinking and Neurological Positivism: Further Elucidations and Implications.* Systems Research: Volume 7 Number 1, 1990. Pergamon Press, New York, USA.

Vickers, Geoffry. 1970. *Freedom in a Rocking Boat Changing Values in an Unstable Societ.* Penguin, Baltimore, USA

Vickers, Sir Geoffrey. 1970. *Freedom in a Rocking Boat. Changing Values in an Unstable Society.* Penguin, Baltimore.

Volume12 Number 3 September 1995 pp. 217-22.

Warfield, John N. 1976. *Societal Systems. Planning, Policy and Complexity.* John Wiley & Sons, New York, USA.

Warfield, John N. 1976. *Societal Systems. Planning, Policy and Complexity.* John Wiley & Sons, New York, USA.

Wellburn, Alan. 1988. *Air Pollution and Acid Rain.* Longman Scientific & Technical, Longman Group UK Limited, Essex, England.

Whitehead, Alfred North. 1919. *The Concept of Nature.* London: Cambridge University Press.

Whitehead, Alfred North. 1925. *Science and the Modern World*, New York: Free Press

Whitehead, Alfred North. 1929. *Process and Reality.* The Free Press, A Division of MacMillan Publishing Co. Inc. Corrected Edition 1978, New York, USA.

Wiener, Norbert. 1954. *The Human Use of Human Beings.* Da capo Press, Inc. A Subsidiary of Plenum Publishing Corporation, New York, USA.

World Development Report *Development and the Environment.* Oxford University Press. Oxford, UK. 1992.

World Development Report *Infrastructure for Development.* Oxford University Press. Oxford, UK, 1994.

World Development Report. 1992. *Development and Environment.* The International Bank for Reconstruction and Development, Oxford University Press. Oxford, England

World Development Report. *Development and the Environment,* 1992. pp. 5, 35, 40

Worldwatch Institute Norden. 1991. *State of the World '91.* Worldwatch Institute, Washington, USA.

Zeigler, Bernhard P. and Weinberg Roger. 1970. *System Theoretic Analysis of Models: Computer Simulation of a Living Cell* Journal of Theoretical Biology, Volume 29, Number 1 October 1970.

REFERENCES INTERNET

http://www.scb.se
Statistics Sweden

http://www.lib.kth.se/~lg/envsite.htm
Environmental Sites on the Internet

http://www.oecd.org/std/hot/gov/
oecd Main Economic Indicators Hot File

http://www.oecd.org/publications/figures/
OECD in Figures 1999

http://europa.eu.int/en/comm/eurostat/serven/part3/euroind/eur11key.htm
EURO indicators Key indicators of the Monetary Union

http://www.oecd.org/std/dnm/STDKei.htm
Statistics at theOECD

http://www.un.org/Depts/unsd/social/main.htm
Capital cities and cities of 100.000 and more inhabitants

http://www.uni-duisburg.de/duisburg/yearbook.htm
International Yearbook of Large Cities Statistics

http://www.odci.gov/cia/publications/factbook/index.html
The World Factbook 1999

http://www.stats.demon.nl/top25.htm
Charts. Countries with the largest population

http://www.wri.org/sdis/data_tbl/
World Resources Data Tables

http://www.worldbank.org/data/databytopic/databytopic.html
The World Bank Group

http://www.census.gov/ipc/www/idbnew.html
U.S. Census Bureau

http://www.fedstats.gov/programs/environ.html
Programs FedStats A to Z Search Fast Facts MapStats SiteMap

http://www.epa.gov/oar/oarhome.html
EPA United StatesEnvironmental Protection Agency

http://europa.eu.int/en/comm/eurostat/facts/wwwroot/en/index.htm
Statistical Office of the European Communities. facts through figures

http://www.iea.org/stats/files/keystats/stats_98.htm
International Energy Agency. Key World Energy Statistics from the IAEA

INDEX

A

B

C

D

E

F

G

H

I

O

P

Q

R

S

T